THE LIBRARY OF
PHILOSOPHY AND THEOLOGY
Edited by
JOHN MCINTYRE and IAN T. RAMSEY

A DIALOGUE OF RELIGIONS

THE LIBRARY OF PHILOSOPHY AND THEOLOGY

Titles in the Series

A DIALOGUE OF
RELIGIONS

NINIAN SMART

*Lecturer in the History and Philosophy of Religion,
King's College, London*

GREENWOOD PRESS, PUBLISHERS
WESTPORT, CONNECTICUT

Library of Congress Cataloging in Publication Data

Smart, Ninian, 1927-
    A dialogue of religions.

    Reprint of the ed. published by SCM Press,
London, which was issued in series: The Library of
philosophy and theology.
    Includes index.
    1. Religions. I. Title.
BL425.S6 1981   291   79-8730
ISBN 0-313-22187-1 (lib. bdg.)

To My Isabels

© SCM Press Ltd. 1960.

First published 1960.

Reprinted with the permission of SCM Press Ltd.

Reprinted from an original copy in the collection of
Penfield Library, State University of New York at
Oswego.

Reprinted in 1981 by Greenwood Press
A division of Congressional Information Service, Inc.
88 Post Road West, Westport, Connecticut 06881

Printed in the United States of America

10 9 8 7 6 5 4 3 2 1

CONTENTS

PREFACE

THE characters in the ensuing Dialogue are: a Christian, a Jew, a Muslim, a Hindu, a Buddhist from Ceylon and a Japanese Buddhist. These are referred to in the text as, respectively: C, J, M, H, CB, and JB.

In order to explain the reasons for writing this Dialogue and to place it in a context, I have included a short Introduction. Also, to help those who are unfamiliar with some of the Eastern terms and names which occur in the text, I have appended a brief Glossary.

In preparing the book I have been helped by Dr Geoffrey Parrinder and by Mr John Olford, both of whom read the manuscript and gave me valuable advice, and by the Rev. David Edwards, who has censored some of my stylistic inelegancies. I am most grateful to them.

The resultant Dialogue still retains crudities, but I console myself by reflecting that some at least are unavoidable in treating of so vast and subtle a subject, and that the brevity of this book may be an advantage which outweighs such blemishes.

N. S.

INTRODUCTION

THIS dialogue of living religions is relevant both to philosophical reflection and to the comparative study of religion. This is why.

There is a narrowness in modern theology and religious philosophy. Sometimes it is argued that reasoning cannot bring us to truth in religion, so that we have to fall back upon revelation. Revelation here is to be appropriated by faith— a faith which sometimes looks as though it is quite hostile to reason. Such a standpoint makes theology dogmatic, and philosophy sterile.

Perhaps, however, theology ought to be dogmatic. Isn't that what it is meant to be? And perhaps too philosophy's ultimate and heartrending task is to show its own bankruptcy as a source of metaphysical truth.

Yet there is an obvious and shattering objection to the narrow appeal to revelation. *Revelations are many.* The Hindu theologian could use the same argument for faith in revelation as does the Christian. If revelations are many, how can we choose between them? Why make the Christian leap of faith, rather than the Muslim or Buddhist one? The case is like that of the Existentialist who cries 'Decide! Make a decision!': very edifying, but decide *what*? Pep talks have their place, but we want guidance as well. The ringing demand that we should believe is answered by the complaint that preachers preach different things. If there is revealed truth, we need to see the reasons for one formulation rather than another.

For this reason, philosophers of religion (that is, all men who think about religion) cannot ignore the comparative study of religions.

But it may be objected that the formulations do not matter: the ultimate truth in all religion is inexpressible. There is substance in this thought. But it is surprising how often those who say this go on to speak about religion, and in terms of the formulations of their own faith! Besides, though ultimately we

9

may all arrive at the ineffable, we start with assertions. Do we seriously believe that all these are on a par? Can I say with impunity that it does not matter at all whether I start as a polytheist or a pantheist or a monotheist?

Or it may be objected that revelation is not a series of propositions supposedly true, but rather the activity of God in breaking through the universe and confronting us personally. No doubt this is true. Yet the very statement of the contrast contains a formulation. 'Revelation is God's activity'—what a wealth of statements is already contained in these words! And it remains, therefore, to ask whether these are the right words to use. They are not quite the words a Hindu or a Buddhist would employ.

Nor can we say that the great religions all really teach the same thing, if we are to go by the words enshrining their beliefs. If words mean anything here, there are different teachings (though also we find illuminating agreements). If words do not mean anything here, then let us forget about doctrines altogether. This is the death of the theologian. More importantly, it is the death of belief. For that which cannot be expressed in any way whatsoever cannot be believed. The meaningless cannot be a creed.

Perhaps we have been deceived partly by modern developments in philosophy. The Verificationists in their hey-day were happy to say that religious statements are meaningless. For these statements (the central ones, at least) cannot be verified or falsified through ordinary observation. This brought about the eerie situation where the Christian kept saying, 'But my assertions about God *are* meaningful—obscure if you like, but meaningful nonetheless'; while the sophisticated agnostic said, 'No, they're meaningless.' It sounded as though St Anselm's 'I believe in order that I may understand' had a very special force. Now if one party to a discussion refuses to agree that what the other fellow says has any meaning, there cannot be a discussion. This leads to the illusion (born of the curious assumption that all religious arguments are between agnostics and believers) that there is no such thing as a religious argument.

Even the current contemporary philosophical movement sometimes called Linguistic Analysis betrays signs of this irrationalism. For it is an easy thing to talk about 'religious language' as though this simply consists in the formulations of the Christian Church. After all, if we do our analysis in a European language, then it is natural to identify religious language with the dominant faith of the Western tribe. It is also natural to forget that the faith of the West has been hammered out on the anvil of heresy; and heretics were usually religious men (misguided, if you like, but in a religious way). Do we really believe that religion consists in a monolithic revelation, single and unarguable? The supposition is plainly absurd.

It is therefore vitally important for the reflective person (poor fellow: how enlightenment is a two-edged sword!) to consider the principles and insights upon which we guide our faith. These matters are brought out sharply by the question, 'Why be a Christian rather than a Buddhist?' No doubt for most people it is not quite a live option, this choice. We are not all of the beatnik generation, pondering Zen. Yet, in regard to truth and understanding, the question must be important. We could dress it up more pompously by saying: 'What are the criteria of truth regarding revelations?' Or even we could put it by saying: 'What are the reasons for faith?'

Or we could bring all this out by saying that in a way religion is grounded and centred upon experiences of certain kinds. The revelations of Allah through Muhammad, the enlightenment of the Buddha, the conversion of St Paul—how central such experiences are in the growth of a religion! Revelation here is presented in the experiences of certain men. More humbly too, it is the experience of ordinary folk that makes the living truth of religion obvious to them. The appeal to revelation itself, a most admirably vision-laden procedure, is in effect an appeal to certain experiences. Yet is it right to stay always within our own tradition? If religious experience is our ground of faith, then let us not be so narrow as to consider only the experiences of *our* tradition.

But, someone perchance will say, it is in *my* experience that

I see Truth. It is in *my* experience that God reveals himself to me. Existentially, I feel that 'I can no other'. Yes, or religion is no live thing. But we *interpret* our experience. We clothe our intuitions in the vestments of one tradition. Sometimes quite unconsciously. Who has seen the Virgin in Banaras? What Sicilian saint or Scotch divine has seen the celestial Buddha? To be reflective (and to be reflective is to be fair, though not to the exclusion of commitment and loving insight) the appeal to experience has to be viewed against the wider backcloth of the great religions.

Nor can we escape the insistent and hammering questions of the world's great faiths by turning to natural theology—that is, by turning to some straightforward rational proofs of the central truths of religion. Although in modern times philosophers for good (though not always overwhelming) reasons have been exceedingly sceptical of the validity of the traditional 'proofs' of God's existence, there are some, notably the followers of St Thomas Aquinas, who regard them as showing something. Yet even here there is trouble. First, because revealed theology still remains, distinguished from natural theology (it being absurd to suppose that the unaided intellect can think out the Trinity doctrine, for example). And if in part we appeal to revelation, then all the questions we have raised recur. Second, and in any case, some Indian theologians, for instance, have used 'proofs' similar to those of the West, but with notably different *theological* results. The great Śaṅkara believes in a First Cause, but the way this First Cause is described would be unacceptable (or at least exceedingly strange) to most Christians. In short, if natural theology says: 'There is something—but as to the details, look to revelation', then we still need to say something about the reasons for accepting *this* revelation.

Thus the purpose of the dialogue which follows is not to settle abstruse philosophical questions about Prime Movers and Necessary Beings. It is, rather, to show the kinds of considerations—the reasons—which are relevant in religious discussions. It is to show how the great religions can differ and agree upon principles, even where it is revelation with which we are dealing.

But the purpose of the dialogue is not to *settle* issues—to show how Christianity must be true or false, or how any other religion must be. It is not apologetics.

To my mind, a trouble with apologetics is that it tends furiously to leap into the fray, without wondering what the rules of combat are. Conversely, the trouble with a peaceable 'We-all-say-the-same-thing-at-bottom' approach is that it sleepily and too good-naturedly evades the question of what the rules of *agreement* are. No wonder that students of religions have hastily retreated into catalogues of facts: 'Hinduism is thus and thus, and as for the questions at the end about truth, well, gentlemen, they're not my province.' All this as if the alternatives are odious comparisons and mere encyclopedias! Sometimes in this way a sinister phenomenon occurs (we are all guilty, no doubt)—the tendency to distort the other faith under the guise of mere description. (One is reminded of the way Englishmen sometimes react when told about American salaries: 'Yes, but the cost of living is higher there, you know'— as though this settles the question.) This distorting temptation is doubtless born of our laudable eagerness to believe our own beliefs, and we feel uneasy if the Buddhist, say, may seem to disagree with these beliefs. 'He doesn't believe in an immortal soul? Now come, my dear chap! If you read the Pāli canon attentively you will see that he really does, or that the Buddha did: of course, he explains it a bit differently. . . .'

Sometimes it is said that if you *believe*, you *must* be biassed. Maybe. But there are degrees of bias, and truth is a duty. All men are sinful, but this does not justify us in having an orgy of sin. Likewise though as religious believers we may be biassed or 'committed', we should be as understanding as possible regarding other faiths, and not make commitment an excuse for prejudice. The same is true, in a slightly different way, if we are agnostics. Still, the objection does indicate that perfection is not to be expected in this sort of enquiry. Yet I have attempted to be as clear and fair in this dialogue as I can.

The demand for fairness is one reason for the dialogue form. It helps us to put ourselves in the other man's shoes. And, of course, it also cuts out all the tiresome paraphernalia of 'To this the Buddhist might object . . .' and 'But the Hindu might reply that . . .'

The dialogue form also emphasizes anew the point that where there is discussion, there reasons are found. The possibility of argument implies that there are criteria of truth, however vague. Indeed, the man who refuses to argue at all is guilty of slaying truth: both the true and the false perish, and he is reduced to mere expressions of feeling. Admittedly, two men arguing about Rembrandt or Mozart may not be able to *persuade* each other. But there is a distinction between the relevant and the irrelevant; and though personal persuasion may not immediately occur, the discussion is part of a social dialogue which does issue in judgments about truth. Likewise in religion.

Moreover, since philosophical analysis, surely a necessary technique whatever one's views about philosophy's ultimate aims, is concerned at least in part with seeing what counts *for* and *against* assertions, the philosophical analysis of religion must listen to the dialogue of religions.

But enough of justifications. It looks suspicious to give so many grounds for recommending such a dialogue: the author doth protest too much. Yet confusion and obscurity in present-day religious thought may justify the justifications.

Such is the rationale and place of this dialogue.

But in case anyone complains about the participants, that some important religions are excluded, a word on this is wise. I have put in a Christian, a Jew, a Muslim, a Hindu and two kinds of Buddhist. But no Taoist, or Confucianist, or representative of an indigenous African religion; no Sikh, no Jain, no Parsī, no Latter Day Saint. But I think it is fair to say that my participants represent the greatest of the living religions, certainly in point of influence. It would be nice to include everybody, but the dialogue would be intolerably complicated.

An effect of the dialogue may, I hope, be an increased understanding of the East by the West, and conversely. For culture and religion are so closely intertwined, even today. At any rate, one thing is obvious: Kipling was absurd about the twain never meeting. We should not, of course, be so hazy and sentimental as to think that the twain were really one all the time. Still, I like my friends precisely because they don't think my thoughts, and yet I understand them.

But it is—need I repeat?—wrong to expect religious conclusions from the dialogue. But I am sure that we cannot lightly defend any such conclusions that we may come to, or may have come to, without first listening to such a dialogue.

Let us, then, listen.

I

POLYTHEISM AND MONOTHEISM

C (*the Christian*): While we are isolated here, with time on our hands, we have an excellent opportunity to discuss religion, and to find out where our basic agreements and disagreements lie. In my country I find that arguments about religion tend too much to be confined to the dispute between faith and agnosticism; while on the other hand, the relations between the major religions of the world are often obscured by the cultural and political dress in which they are clothed. Wouldn't it be illuminating to see whether we can attain some degree of understanding on the principles, if any, underlying the doctrinal differences between us? But I'd like us to confine ourselves as far as possible to religious issues and not get bogged down in philosophical or metaphysical disputes.

CB (*the Ceylon Buddhist*): I'm not quite clear what you mean by the word 'religion' here. It has often been said, as you know, that my form of Buddhism, Theravāda Buddhism, isn't a religion at all. Sometimes this is even said about Buddhism as a whole. The point of such a remark is that in the Theravāda there's no way to salvation which depends on the grace of God —indeed, the worship of God does not figure in it. And so, if 'religion' is defined as a system which bends men to the will of God or the gods, then the definition would probably exclude those teachings where a belief in gods or spirits is merely marginal—as in the Theravāda and in the Sāṅkhya school of Hinduism. It's for this reason that the word 'philosophy' is sometimes used to characterize such systems of doctrine.

C: I'm glad you raised the point. But with your permission I shall extend the use of the word 'religion' beyond its etymology, so that it covers systems of salvation, whether or not such salvation is specifically described by reference to God or gods. It is because the Buddha preached *salvation* that I don't want to call his teachings a philosophy. In this respect, of course, I'm thinking of philosophy in a typically Western way: but since we're speaking English it makes for clarity to do so. What I thought we ought to exclude from our discussion was purely *metaphysical* argument—like the so-called proofs of the existence of God, of the immortality of the soul, and so on—so that we could avoid what might turn out to be an interminable series of intellectual disputes. Also, this restriction on our discussion accords with a principle which I hold dear; namely, that religion, to be real religion, must be a matter of experience. I am more interested in the Viṣṇu of devotional Hinduism than I am in Aristotle's Prime Mover! That's why I don't wish to speak seriously of Epicureanism as a religion, for there the gods live quite apart from men and have no relations with them. Indeed, perhaps it's even wrong to call them 'gods'. So with your approval I'd like to talk about living religion and try to see what real religious reasons we may have for agreeing or differing amongst ourselves.

CB: I find your programme congenial, but I was wondering how some of the others would feel. I was even thinking that you, as a Christian, were not really in a position to have such a discussion. Don't you believe in a revelation of or by God? Isn't *this* the test of truth? Is there any further argument?

C: You think that my attitude is rather empirical? Rather Buddhist, shall we say? It is—in the sense that it's not sufficient in my view, to label something 'Revelation'. I believe in revelation not because it is said to be revelation, but because it bears the marks of a true revelation. Moreover, in the middle of the twentieth century, Christianity is confronted as never before by imposing and profound rivals, such as your own Buddhism. Do you think that I want to be an ostrich, and bury my head in sands of blind faith? Surely, if I'm to remain a Christian, I must have reason to think that my own faith gives a better picture of spiritual realities. To this extent, then, my religious views are empirical. They *have* to be!

H (*the Hindu*): I take it that you aren't using 'empirical' in any technical or philosophical sense, and that you don't want us simply to stick to what can be said in terms of sense-experience. Indeed, you spoke of experience as though you were meaning *religious* experience. But surely there are different types of experiences connected with religion?

C: There are, I'm sure. But, since we must make a beginning somewhere, I will ask this question—*what is it that makes men believe in gods?*

J (*the Jew*): Did you say God or gods? None of us here would wish, I hope, to be called polytheists—though I confess that to me Hinduism seems to allow polytheism. And the same goes for Mahāyāna Buddhism, with all its talk of Buddhas and Bodhisattvas. Even Christianity, I fear, isn't free from suspicion on this score (I'm not just thinking of the cult of saints and all that, which might perhaps be defended and which in any event isn't found throughout Christendom: no, I'm thinking of the Trinity doctrine itself). My Muslim friend here will doubtless be with me in refusing to countenance what are—to put it bluntly—blasphemous beliefs and practices. It doesn't seem to me that we can discuss the experience of the one pure God in the same breath as those other experiences men may have which they describe by reference to gods—gods which are really things of nought.

C: I'm interested that, even if you condemn some of us for polytheistic tendencies, you recognize that none of us would wish to be *called* polytheists. This indicates that you believe we are secretly agreed on some principle here: that belief in one God is somehow better than belief in many.

H: It's true, of course, that the Hindu view of the matter allows that polytheism is a legitimate form of religion, even though the highest truth may be that there is but one Ultimate Reality. Why do we say this? We believe that not all people are at the same stage of spiritual development. The village woman who lays flowers before a tree or before what you would misleadingly call an 'idol' is expressing here a religious sense, though at a comparatively low level and within the limits of her understanding. And our scriptures do in fact often suggest that Brahman, the Supreme Reality, pervades everything. So there is, we believe, a way in which the village woman, in discerning a spirit in the tree, is seeing a fragment, though only a fragment, of the one sacred Reality.

C: These are points which we'll have to return to later. Let's note, however, that this idea of 'stages of development' is a bit different from our view. For though we, as Christians, believe that God has educated His people up to the supreme revelation in Christ, this is an *historical* development—whereas yours is an *educational* development. You think of people as being at different stages of spiritual education, here and now: but we think of the education as having occurred in the history of the race (in the history, especially, of the Chosen People). Perhaps it is easier for you to have this tolerant educational theory when you also believe in rebirth, for there is not the same terrible urgency about getting people to see the highest truth. And certainly also, as you've said, pantheism is more accommodating in respect of local deities and so on.

JB (*the Japanese Buddhist*): J suggested that we of the Great Vehicle are polytheists because we pray to many Bodhisattvas and celestial Buddhas, who are as numerous as the sands of the Ganges. Yet of course all Buddhas are one in their *dharmakāya* or Truth-Body, which is the same as Ultimate Reality. If you like, all Buddhas are in essence one, and this Essence is Ultimate Reality. All the Buddhas are but manifestations of the one Absolute. In this way we preserve the ordinary worshipper's feeling for the numinous, without however wishing to concede that the forms under which such beings are worshipped are the basic expression of Reality. In this, I'm much in sympathy with the characteristic Hindu view. And I'll add that though Gautama, at the stage of development which men had reached in his day, did not preach the adoration of celestial Buddhas as a help towards insight and release, nevertheless he treated ordinary religion, on the whole, with silent respect. It was only bad where it kept men from a higher way.

C: Still, we seem to be agreed that the *highest* truth is that there's only one great Being; but some of us refuse to countenance anything like polytheism as a form of 'lower' truth. Perhaps this amounts basically to a difference in emphasis upon the importance of preserving the purity of worship. For I at least, though I come from an 'anti-polytheistic' group of religions stemming from ancient Judaism, would admit that even in polytheism there are intimations of the one 'unknown God'. I'd agree with H that the village woman has some inkling perhaps of the Divine Majesty. But I say that her view of God is terribly defective.

H: Yes, you certainly do place great emphasis on having the correct view, the right formula of belief. There I differ from you—since I tend to think of *all* views of God as essentially defective!

J: But so do we all! But surely some views are better—almost immeasurably better—than others. And surely what we're trying to do now is to find some way of seeing why one view might be superior to another—though I confess that the manifest guidance and help given by God to Israel makes me feel a certain unrealism in this discussion.

C: I think we've so far agreed on at least this point, that basically monotheism or pantheism is better than polytheism. But precisely why do we think this?

M (*the Muslim*):   There's no need to ask. The unity of the Godhead is something which those who have been his vessels of revelation unhesitatingly affirm. This is the core of the teaching of Muḥammad and the other Prophets.

C: Perhaps I've been corrupted by the work of our modern Christian theologians, my friend, but I wouldn't be quite so bold as to affirm that in God's revelation of himself to the individual, He writes His own name and attributes across the experience. The words with which revelation is expressed themselves seem to be a kind of interpretation. To suppose that God literally speaks words to the Prophets seems in itself a blasphemous anthropomorphism. This is where I find your attitude to the Qu'rān hard to understand.

M: Well, I don't know what to say. But I don't want to wreck the discussion by insisting on our fundamentalist approach. Perhaps I can appeal to some of our mystics and philosophers to excuse myself for remaining within this conversation.

C: Perhaps we can agree on this: that the more over-whelming and pure the numinous experience is, the more natural it is to speak of it as the self-revelation of a Supreme Being. And I take it that we can distinguish between the more 'primitive' and fragmentary experiences of the numinous and those which are more intense and exalted? It's perhaps difficult to characterize this sort of difference, but don't you think it can be recognized?

M: I suppose so. I would wish to point to such men as Moses and the Prophet as instances of those who have had such overwhelming insight. And I think you'd agree that this Supreme Power who reveals Himself thus is due the pro-foundest worship. This is why we are truly slaves of Allah.

H: The deeper experiences, then, within the context of worship tend in the direction of monotheism. This can be well illustrated from the *Bhagavadgītā*, with its amazing and wonderful theophany, and its emphasis on devotion to the Supreme Lord.

C: And I suppose that as well as being more pure and exalted, belief in one God is simpler than belief in many. Other things being equal, a simple belief has an inherently greater attraction than a complicated one. This rather formal point may strike you as cold and lifeless. But remember that chaotic legends about many gods, as well as not always being edifying, can leave one in an unhappy perplexity.

J: You mustn't forget either that our God is truly trans-cendent, whereas there's always doubt about this regarding particular deities. For instance, though the divinity of a Sun-God may not be simply observable in the face of the sun, the sun, even *qua* god, is contained within the cosmos. I consider this transcendence of God as of the utmost importance. Any other view is blasphemous.

H: Isn't *any* false view about divine matters blasphemous? Saying that any other view than the one you believe is blasphemous is, in the context of religious worship, just another way of saying that it is false. Now our picture of Brahman as, in a way, pantheistic, will no doubt also be condemned by you as blasphemous. But what are the canons of blasphemy? How are we to determine what is blasphemous and what isn't?

J: 'My ways are not thy ways,' saith the Lord. Anything which serves to minimize the absolute Otherness of the Divine Being is a failure to ascribe to Him His due glory, majesty and awefulness.

H: And you say that this Otherness is perceived in the experience of the numinous? The reason why I ask is that there's a great deal said in Hinduism about being deified, about becoming Brahman. Brahman and the Self (what you might call the soul) are in some sense one, at least according to one influential interpretation of the scriptural teachings. Thus we don't necessarily wish to stress to the same degree the vast difference between God and man. Are we being blasphemous in asserting that in the higher flight of mystical experience one can, so to speak, become merged with God?

JB: For us too, though the way of devotion to the Tathāgata is religiously fruitful, there isn't that absolute difference between worshipper and God which theism implies. For we are all capable of enlightenment in the long run and so of uniting ourselves in the *dharmakāya* with Ultimate Reality. The Buddha-nature resides in each one of us. In worshipping the Buddha we are paying reverence to our own future condition!

M: I'm indeed reminded of the more extreme pronouncements of our Ṣūfīs—like the one who said: 'I am the Real'. And if I mistake not, Meister Eckhart wasn't far off the

Advaitin view. But I am unhappy about the orthodoxy of such contemplatives: or perhaps it is that their way of expressing themselves is sometimes unfortunate, and very disturbing for the ordinary faithful worshipper.

H: There's something of a paradox here. For while theists want to emphasize the great gulf fixed between God and man, they nevertheless ascribe attributes, in particular personal attributes, to God. Roughly, the personal Deity of Judaism and Islam seems to correspond to our *Īśvara*, the Lord. Now in Śaṅkara's system, for example, this Lord is merely a lower aspect of the Godhead. It's true that not all theologians and saints in Hinduism are agreed on this, and that some of our writings, notably the *Bhagavadgītā*, are distinctly theistic in spirit. Yet there's a strong strand in our theology which claims that the higher aspect of God is without attributes of the kind that you ascribe to God, and that the lower aspect is, in effect, useful for the purposes of worship but in the highest truth a product of illusion. For if the world itself is illusory, then the picture of God as creator and sustainer of the cosmos must be infected with illusion. The paradox then is this: that in one way at least non-theistic doctrine may express more forcibly the Otherness of God.

C: I don't agree that this is a paradox, for it's been wrongly put. It's primarily in the *numinous* experience—the experience which grows out of worship and the submission of oneself to God—that the notion of His Otherness arises. It's the contrast between the unholy, unclean, puny sinner and the terrible, holy, pure, majestic Godhead that gives us an inkling of His transcendence. Now if this Being whom we encounter in worship and prostration appears to have personal character-istics (and don't the great prophets and teachers speak thus?), it's not surprising that theists ascribe to Him such personal attributes! But my main point is that the notion of Otherness is yielded by this kind of experience—the sort that Job had when he wished to clothe himself in dust and ashes and which one of your Hindu saints had when he cried that he was a cur and that it was sinful to think of any creature as Viṣṇu. There is much of this too behind the Greek idea of *hubris*: it is *hubris* to pretend to be god-like.

H: How, then, is Hinduism unsatisfactory?

C: In this way, I think. The attributes of Being, Consciousness and Bliss which the Hindu non-dualist ascribes to the impersonal Godhead are also attributes of the immortal Self *within* each one of us. So Śaṅkara's system hardly expresses that Otherness which theism so forcibly does. It's indeed typical of the mystical experience that there should be difficulty in distinguishing between subject and object (as the matter is often put), and so there arises a sense of merging with God or the Absolute. This is a special kind of religious experience which is different, I think, from the numinous experience of the worshipper. I know this is a very crude way of describing the situation, but perhaps you understand what I'm getting at. I'd like to propose the working hypothesis, which we can discuss later if you like, that the mystical experience has a distinctive connection with the more 'impersonalist' doctrines, such as those of Advaita Vedānta and of certain forms of Buddhism. But of that more anon.

H: I still don't understand this business about 'blasphemy'!

C: A false view of the Holy Being *is* blasphemous; and to call a view blasphemous from within the sphere of worship and adoration is to indicate its falsity. Blasphemy arises because liturgy and doctrine can hardly be disentangled, and wrong doctrine is a case of taking God's name in vain.

M: But to call a view merely 'false' isn't to express any forcible condemnation. Aren't you being too soft?

C: To call an attitude to baseball wrong-headed isn't a severe castigation; to call an attitude to morals wrong-headed is a much more serious matter. And why? Because the seriousness of error is proportionate to the importance of the subject-matter. Since we're here dealing with religion, admittedly the most vital and solemn of matters, to call a view false is already a severe condemnation. (But there is a difference between saying that a view is blasphemous and that a person is.) What I'm leading up to, though, is that I think H is right: J needs to say more in defence of the transcendence of God than that other views are blasphemous, for he's here merely repeating in another way that God is in truth transcendent.

J: But isn't God's transcendence an aspect, so to speak, of His *holiness*? Perhaps that's what I was trying to say. I mentioned a belief in particular deities as somehow terribly defective. They're defective because these gods are *contained* in the cosmos.

CB: Why shouldn't they be? We're quite happy, in our form of Buddhism, to recognize the gods and spirits as inhabitants of the cosmos. They're strange and superior beings (in some ways), but like the rest of beings in the world they are ultimately impermanent. But then perhaps I oughtn't to intervene here, since you gentlemen are speaking so much about worship, and this doesn't appear as an important or central constituent of our faith. Of course, ordinary folk have processions, and at first glance our temples look a bit like places of worship. But at bottom these popular practices are just ways of expressing our reverence for the departed (and human) Master. So perhaps you'll let me raise a general query about the necessity of worship later.

H: Still, CB's question was a good one. Why *shouldn't* the gods be contained within the universe?

J: I believe that I can give some sort of answer to that—if you all agree that, as has been said earlier, intense numinous experiences point in the direction of monotheism. As a generalization from this: the more overwhelming the numinous experience, the more exalted the divinity intimated by it—the limiting case being a monotheistic Deity. Now if there is warrant in the lives of the Prophets and others for belief in such a Being, we should reject the idea of finite gods as grossly inadequate. But in addition, this one Lord in whom we believe is, by his very holiness, concealed: not just behind some particular object like the sun, but behind this whole wide world. Such a

Supreme Being is, as we put it crudely, 'beyond space and time'.
Thus the intensity of religious experience seems to point un-
mistakably in the direction of a truly transcendent Being. I feel
it hard to keep His holiness and His transcendence apart. So
the notion of finite deities contained in the universe is somehow
doubly inconsistent with the holiness of the one Lord. And I
agree with the objection that in polytheism the many gods often
conflict with one another and acquire intractable clusters of
local legend. And they often act so outrageously!

CB: Perhaps the immorality of the gods indicates their
transcendence of moral laws?

J: Well, that may be a sort of defence of polytheism, but a
pretty desperate one, I'd have thought. One would expect that
true transcendence would consist in being *more* perfect, not less
perfect, than men. Pure monotheism manages to integrate the
insights of religion and conscience in a wonderful way: the
God we worship is also perfectly good.

H: There's much in what you say there. But perhaps we
have been at cross-purposes about the concealment of the holy.
For I want to say that, as some of our scriptures put it,
Brahman *is* 'all this'. It is this universe, because It is the Reality
of reality, the essence, as it were, of all this world, concealed
within it everywhere. Hence a god contained within the world,
who hides in the sun or the moon or a rain-cloud, can be looked
on not too implausibly as a fragment of Brahman: or rather,
let's say that those who speak as if there are many gods, as
though the world is full of spirits, aren't too far off the truth.

J: But they are still *off* the truth?

H: Yes: theirs is only a preliminary attempt to portray this
truth, but one can rise beyond such a picture.

J: We've returned to the point where we were before, when
we saw how you have something like 'education by gradualism'
in Hinduism. We on the other hand do not get people to see the
truth by educating them *through* polytheism, but by getting
them to repudiate it.

M: Yes, we fear too much the corruption involved in worshipping gods rather than the True God.

C: Let's pause a moment. So far we've agreed that monotheism and pantheism are superior to polytheism, for various reasons. Let me try and sum them up. First, the intensity of certain revelations or numinous experiences points in the direction of monotheism. Second, and connectedly, the idea of discrete divinities, often clashing, hardly matches up to the overwhelming and pure nature of certain theophanies. Third, someone mentioned local legends: is it not rather characteristic of polytheism to attach itself to particular places, like Olympus? And this would prevent it from becoming a universal religion, and thus offends our feeling that the truth is one for all peoples. Fourth, the stories about the gods are far from edifying. And then, too, we might call in history and say that we do find a certain drift from polytheism towards a unified conception. This is in accordance with the point I made, that a simple belief (other things being equal) is rightly more attractive than a complicated one.

H: I think I agree with all this. But I would add that mystical experience itself indicates a single Ultimate Reality which can be realized in some way (let us not quarrel for the moment about how we're to formulate the matter) within the depths of the soul. But there still remains the difference between us about education, spiritual education.

M: Can I mention another point relevant before we go on to the education question? Though you wanted us to steer clear of metaphysics, surely we ought to consider the thought that the existence of the cosmos demands a First Cause, or something.

CB: Does it? The Buddha told us to avoid such questions, as being a snare and a delusion and not conducive to salvation. When you're struck by a missile you don't delay medical attention until you've found out the name of the man who is responsible. As to the eternity of the world, and all such

27

questions, the Buddha gave no answer. They are 'undetermined' questions.

C: Still, while I can't help admiring the strange and wonderful simplicity of the Buddha's teachings and his acute concentration upon the cure for our ills, there's no denying that men have also felt astonishment that anything does exist, that there is a cosmos. Of course I recognize that the traditional arguments for God's existence do not appear inescapably valid. But it's reasonable to say that the 'cosmological astonishment' is something of a religious feeling, and so comes within our present purview.

H: We could compromise by saying that this feeling of unease as to why the cosmos exists at all constitutes a motive for monotheism or monistic pantheism, but that it couldn't, so to speak, supply us with a belief in one Being had we not already had experiences or revelations of such a Being. Religious thought is primary: metaphysical argument is secondary.

C: All right, let's compromise on that, even if there's a great deal more to be said on this which we can't go into now. So far, then, we've sketched out some religious reasons, which relate to religious experience (and indeed moral experience, if the distinction may be allowed) for thinking that belief in one Being is nearer the truth than polytheism, assuming that we allow validity to the numinous experience. On this last point, we'll leave over till later the objection that CB has brought— namely, that we have been busily talking upon the assumption that worship is a centrally important religious activity, while the Theravāda relegates this very much to the background, and states its central doctrine of salvation in terms of inner illumination, without connecting this to anything we would call God or even Ultimate Reality. Meanwhile, there remains the disagreement between us over our attitude to polytheism. Monism and pantheism are more hospitable to the latter than Christians, Muslims or Jews are. I suspect too that the Indian educational theory about religion is connected in some way with the common Eastern belief in rebirth, which makes both religious and secular problems seem less pressing.

CB: Perhaps you're not generous enough here. Isn't it also that there's greater doctrinal tolerance in Hinduism and Buddhism? This, for instance, is one of the marked features of Buddhism, that there isn't the same drive to impose religious uniformity upon adherents. And we don't go in for religious wars!

J: Yes, but remember that it's our burning vision of one Holy Lord which impels us to denounce in such strong terms the polytheistic tendencies and practices in other faiths. Hence, by way of corollary, our desire to say that the Lord is *beyond* or *outside* the visible world, though philosophically it may be difficult to distinguish from the idea that He is *within* everything, is at least less likely to lead to a toleration of idolatry.

H: Yet there may be other considerations favouring monism as in our systems of belief. For instance, the Advaita view that there is only one Reality, which you can find by turning away from the illusory world, which is only a product of Ignorance—this picture of the world and of Reality is born of mystical insight, in the interior vision which is the blissful cognition of Brahman.

C: I'm aware that some Christians have come near to speaking in a similar way, as when Eckhart said that the world is a mere nothing, though such ways of speaking don't sound really orthodox. But perhaps we can agree that monotheism is the highest form of the religion of worship, other things being equal. You yourself, H, must know well how some Hindu theologians, under the influence of *bhakti* devotionalism, have come very close to our conception of God.

H: But earlier you said we should pay close attention to experience. And it seems to me sufficient that we should adopt the attitude of *bhakti* without saying that the personal manifestation of the Godhead, such as Viṣṇu, exhausts the truth about the Supreme Being. Mystical experience may produce a different emphasis altogether.

C: All I'm for the moment wanting to say is that, as far as the religion of worship and devotion is concerned, other things being equal, personal monotheism is the highest conception.

JB: Yes, some of our Jōdo pietists have hinted that loving personality is, so to speak, at the heart of the Absolute. This I suppose is not unconnected with the devotionalism of such Mahāyāna sects. I myself wouldn't subscribe precisely to such a view, and I'm not sure that it's characteristic of the Mahāyāna as a whole, even if the Great Vehicle does place quite a lot of emphasis upon piety.

C: Right, then, I'll take it that we're agreed upon something like a conditional principle, namely that by reference to the experiences of the numinous and to the related religion of worship and adoration, monotheism is the limiting case; and it is the highest form of such religion. But there may be other reasons for saying that it's not the highest truth, and we'll come to these later. However, we have come up against two difficulties in our discussion which we ought to settle before we go any further. The first is that there's some disagreement about the nature of human life. While we of the Judaic tradition view this life as the only one which the individual can live in this visible world, the rest of us believe, in varying ways, in the doctrine of rebirth. And this is bound to affect our ideas about the urgency of salvation, and thus about how we should view polytheism. It also affects, of course, our views about the *nature* of salvation. The second matter which must be put on the agenda is that raised earlier by CB, when he expressed doubts as to the necessity of a religion of worship at all. This latter involves perhaps a very profound disagreement, but let us leave it for a while and turn first to the problem of rebirth.

II

REBIRTH AND SALVATION

C: It wouldn't be candid of me if I weren't to begin by saying that the doctrine of rebirth, though it has appeared in Western culture among the Greeks and had a limited vogue in the early Church, is really alien to our religion. And, intellectually, it seems hard to accept.

H: But aren't there cases where people seem to recall former lives?

CB: Buddhist saints claim to be able to do this sort of thing.

C: Perhaps my remark was out of place, since we're trying to avoid philosophical disputes. But I think it's nevertheless worth pointing out that belief in rebirth, like belief in miracles, does have reference to what goes on in the observable world, and is therefore more vulnerable to empirical evidence. On the other hand, I don't deny that what you gentlemen call release from the round of rebirth has some independent application. I think that, viewed at least in terms of experience, your *mokṣa* and *nirvāṇa*, despite their conceptual connection with the notion of rebirth (since it is the round of *saṁsāra* that they constitute liberation *from*) might possibly be in their different ways genuine methods of liberation. I'm less opposed to your description of salvation, though even this is sometimes incomplete, than to your affirmation of what it's salvation *from*.

CB: I'm not sure how far one can separate the two aspects, and it's worth realizing that we Hindus and Buddhists don't merely believe in doctrines of rebirth, but ascribe a *cause* to the continued succession of lives. For instance, it's what we Theravādins call *taṇhā* or craving which causes rebirth. Thus *nirvāṇa* is the going out or cooling off of this burning thirst or craving. And on the Hindu non-dualistic view, the cycle of reincarnation is essentially the product of ignorance.

H: Yes, and the two views are very similar in this respect, since ultimately the Buddhists trace back the craving in a succession of causes to ignorance.

M: It does seem odd to think of evil as being due to ignorance, rather than to sin.

H: But it's not ordinary ignorance. Śaṅkara clearly distinguishes between higher and lower truth. The latter is ordinary knowledge, and it is not lack of *this*, but rather lack of knowledge of the higher truth, which causes the trouble. If you like to put it loosely, it's lack of *spiritual* insight which causes men to remain in the grip of ordinary desires and so to remain in the cycle of rebirth.

J: A little while back you complained a bit about the emphasis on having right belief or the right formula of belief in the Judaic religions. It seems paradoxical that you should now say that liberation essentially depends on having the correct *view*!

H: The point is well taken. But remember that with, say, the Christian insistence upon orthodoxy goes a view about man which ascribes his ills to sin. It's but an easy step to saying that wrong belief is sinful, and this is likely to lead to a quite unnecessary rigidity of approach. On the other hand, we would prefer to speak of Original Ignorance (so to say); and although we recognize that liberation comes through the dispelling of this ignorance we aren't so insistent that we have the right formulation of the Truth. This is ultimately beyond words, and has to be experienced.

JB: Here you come close to Zen Buddhism, which shows again how we keep returning to certain fundamental insights.

C: We're also returning to an item in our discussion which I thought we'd disposed of! For though we all see that human language is indeed inadequate for catching the Truth, for describing the Infinite, for doing justice to the beatific vision, yet nevertheless we just have to continue to use words. And though all words may be unsatisfactory, some are less unsatisfactory than others.

JB: Even a Zen Buddhist might concede that! Of course, it's not just the words but the way they're spoken. But I don't wish to insist upon a Zen approach, since it's rather useless discussing it. For the Truth has to be conveyed from master to pupil, and this isn't a matter of intellectual communication such as can be performed through books or lectures. (In view of this, it's surprising how many books there *are* on Zen Buddhism! But I do not mean this too unkindly.) For this reason it might be wise explicitly to exclude Zen from our discussion. However, don't let me divert the course of the argument. I think we can agree that some words are better than others.

C: To return then to rebirth. Isn't it a paradox that while the Christian desires immortality, this is precisely what the Hindu and Buddhist tries to escape?

H: At first sight, it does seem strange. But Hinduism and Buddhism and Christianity are really closer than this would suggest. Remember, you have this Judaeo-Christian picture of a personal Deity, with its reflected evaluation of human beings as important individual persons; your belief in immortality rather involves picturing heaven as a persisting personal life close to God. And in popular imagination, this naturally looks like a continuation of one's earthly career in blissful conditions. This is brought out well too in the descriptions of the Muslim Paradise, which makes it look just like a delectable worldly existence. Now the interesting thing is that whereas we too, and the Buddhists, in our imaginings conceive of heavens and hells, we regard them *as other compartments of the cosmos*—bits which are still under the sway of *karma*. Under favourable conditions you will be reborn in heaven, but this is still in the cycle of rebirth, and ultimately liberation will take you beyond this heavenly condition. So from *our* point of view your heaven or paradise is simply another compartment of the cosmos—and when you talk of eternal life it looks very like our eternal cycle of rebirth! Your immortality looks like our eternal mortality which one has to escape. Put it another way: you think of life as being born, living three score years and ten, and then being translated to another realm; we think of it as being reborn, living a span, dying and being reborn, and so on. It's therefore natural to think of your 'other-worldly' existence as a continuation of what we call the cycle of rebirth.

C: But we *don't* think of heaven just as you describe it. I mean, one has to use pictorial imagery, but . . .

H: I was coming to that. I offered to show that our two views aren't so far apart as the initial paradox suggested. I do recognize that descriptions of heaven aren't to be taken in too literal a fashion. Or if you like to put it this way, it's hard, very hard, to know where to draw the boundary of the cosmos.

JB: Sorry, I don't follow you.

H: Some of the Mahāyāna Buddhists believe in a Paradise far to the West—the 'Pure Land'. Now if this is, so to speak, far enough away to correspond to the Christian or Muslim heaven: if it's far enough away to be where God is—why, then, even though it's supposed, on the Buddhist world-picture, to be part of the universe, it might be plausible to draw a line between it and the visible world and count it as being 'the other world' in the Christian sense. In so far as in the Mahāyāna there's an increasing emphasis on life in Paradise, it becomes assimilated to Christianity. This is rather a complicated topic; but perhaps it prepares the ground for my main point. If we agree that the Christian doesn't want to have his descriptions of heaven taken too literally and that immortality is dwelling with God beyond the grave, then it begins to look like some of our Hindu descriptions of release. If Christian immortality *is* life with God, it's close to the Hindu conception—even if on the non-dualistic view salvation in effect becomes life *in* the Divine Being rather than *with* the Divine Being.

C: Can we sum it up like this? The main difference, from

34

this point of view, between our respective beliefs is that while we Christians think of life as lasting seventy years or so, on the Indian doctrine it lasts a very, very long time.

H: More precisely, there's no limit to human persistence in the world, since one just goes on living and re-living without limit unless something is done about it. I think, by the way, that this view is spiritually advantageous, since the Hindu doesn't have mixed motives regarding survival. It often seems to me that Christians like to believe in immortality, not because they genuinely desire life with God, but simply because they don't like the idea of being snuffed out!

C: I concede that this is often so. Perhaps the point is well brought out by the story of the Presbyterian minister who, hearing that certain modernist theologians were denying the existence of hell, cried: 'Lord, Lord, where now is my hope of immortality?'

J: One at least can admire his humility!

CB: Nevertheless, in the highest kind of life, one must neither desire continued existence nor an end of existence. The saint desires *neither* life *nor* death.

C: And yet provided the desire is for immortality in communion with God, there seems nothing wrong. This is perhaps where a synthesis between the spirit of worship and the sentiments of the mystic shows itself. For by 'renouncing the world'—in the sense that one does everything for the greater glory of God—one comes close, I suspect, to your idea of detachment. Indeed, this is the central insight of the *Bhagavadgītā*. Thus I agree with the Buddha's insistence that our primary motive in religion shouldn't be survival. It should instead be the hope of God's blessing: or rather, the hope of finding beatification in God. In other words, we shouldn't desire immortality because thereby we are not snuffed out, but because the whole logic of the religion of worship is that the Supreme Object of worship is the *summum bonum*. In this way, then, the Hindu and the Christian aren't too far apart; and we

35

can sympathize with the Buddha's dislike of the question as to whether the self is eternal or not.

CB: I'm not sure how far you can do so. Surely it's obvious that the promise of eternal life is bound to mix people's motives? I agree, of course, that any religion is bound to offer *some* higher way, and I don't deny that you'll find in our scriptures arguments to show that one's true interest is to follow the Noble Eightfold Path. The only snag is that the notion of personal immortality directs attention back to one's self, and that's dangerous.

JB: Yet the Great Vehicle has always maintained that you Theravādins, by ignoring the power and good example of the Bodhisattvas, and by concentrating almost exclusively upon the ideal of *arhat*-ship, fell into this very trap. But these are perhaps side-issues in the present context.

C: What we've learned, I think, is that there's no incompatibility in general between the Hindu and Christian idea of eternal life. Where we do disagree is over the duration of this-worldly existence. We must note too that souls are, on the Hindu view, pre-existent. This is, of course, bound up with the whole idea of rebirth. And for the Buddhists too, though there is no permanent Self underlying the empirical states of consciousness and so forth, yet equally there is no limit in time, in either direction, to the process of *karma*—that is, if we exclude the possibility of the escape from it which constitutes *nirvāṇa*.

J: Regarding rebirth, I think that we three of the Judaic faiths will just have to differ with our friends here. But it would be interesting to consider the effects of this difference. You, C, suggested that belief in rebirth was a contributing factor to the greater apparent credal tolerance in Eastern religions.

H: What C had in mind, I imagine, was that there's less *urgency* about salvation where you have plenty of other chances. I suppose that this is true. And perhaps also our belief in rebirth makes us think of salvation as a more strenuous matter— if one is so much entangled in matter that one goes on being reborn again and again it will seem likely that it requires very considerable *effort* to escape! This doesn't entirely account for our tradition of austerities and spiritual exercises of a difficult nature (such as Yoga). But it certainly fits in with this tradition. However, it is not a universal attitude among Hindus that salvation is very hard, since our *bhakti* theologians stress the power of God's grace, so that He does it all for us, if we but love and adore Him.

JB: It's an interesting point, in connection with this, that the fullest flowering of the Mahāyāna took place in China and Japan, where belief in rebirth is not indigenous, and that in these countries there grew up a strong strand of devotional religion, where again it is through the Buddha's grace, or through the bounty of Bodhisattvas in bestowing the treasures of their merit upon unworthy men, that the latter can gain salvation.

C: And would I be right in supposing that belief in rebirth affects Buddhism in the following way, that the early teaching implied that an ordinary layman couldn't attain to *nirvāṇa*? What I mean is that such a doctrine is more palatable where there is rebirth. For otherwise Buddhism is no longer a system of *universal* salvation.

CB: I don't think you've put the point very tactfully. You mustn't think that the belief in rebirth is due to a desire for an exclusively monastic way of salvation. It is simply that we believe in rebirth, and so find it in no way absurd that the ordinary layman cannot reach *nirvāṇa*. The life of the *bhikkhu* is our ideal. But don't you too have monks?

C: I wasn't meaning to suggest that rebirth is some kind of *ad hoc* teaching, but I was trying to show how the whole thing hangs together.

J: I find another very important 'hanging together', which may account for the differing views of history as between East and West. What I had in mind is this: that the doctrine of rebirth is of a piece with the cyclical view of the history of the

37

cosmos. This *saṁsāra*, this everlasting round of beings circling from one condition to another, the remarkable skill with which duration of each successive world is computed, all the proliferation of zeros with which the millions of years in the world's course are adorned—all this suggests a rather different view of history from that implicit in the Judaic faiths! Not so long ago we thought that the world began in 4004 B C or thereabouts. You wouldn't easily have got an Indian believing that! This is to his credit, perhaps. But it indicates a marked difference of viewpoint. And as for the Buddhist, why, he's not ready to commit himself to the belief that the world had a beginning in time at all!

CB: Why should we torture our intellects over something which is hardly relevant to salvation?

J: I was working round to the point that it *is* relevant to salvation, even though the connection mayn't be obvious to start with. It all ties up with our conception of God.

H: And how is this?

J: A little while back we were remarking that there's a 'cosmological uneasiness', a feeling that it's surprising that something exists rather than nothing. We have the feeling that the universe is *contingent*. Now maybe we're wrong in having this feeling. But surely the doctrine that God created the world by an act of will harmonizes gloriously with this contingency. The Lord creates from nothing and sustains continually the cosmos: and if He withdrew His support it would all vanish away in the twinkling of an eye. How does this connect with history? I suggest that the pantheistic or monistic idea, of the First Being evolving in some manner, clothing Itself in the visible world, has a certain air of *necessity* about it. Pantheists hardly feel the awful *contingency* of the world.

H: How do you Jews think about Genesis nowadays?

J: I'd put it like this. We can best express the complete dependence and contingency of the cosmos by thinking of the creation as something like an act of will, and therefore something which is best described in such a story as is found in Genesis. I'm not suggesting that we *make up* the story in order to express ourselves, but that we can perceive in this revelation a peculiar aptness. And though the story of the Creation isn't literal history (how could it be?), it is *analogical* history. It has to be presented *in the guise* of history. And though this is only a guise, it rings true. But perhaps you don't see what I'm driving at.

C: I do, for one. What you are saying is that though the story of the Creation is not literal, but rather analogical, history, it chimes in with the view which we both hold, that God reveals Himself in the sequence of historical events. It harmonizes with the whole grand pageant of God's providential care throughout the course of history, with His guidance given to Israel, with the historical revelation in Christ.

J: M and I will demur on the last item. But you have in general appreciated what I was trying to get at. And the converse of all this is that the emanationist or evolutionary picture of the creation of the world (I'm not, by the way, meaning 'evolutionary' in the modern scientific sense) chimes in better with the cyclical view of history as in Indian religion. This is why I said at the outset that these different views of the world go back to different conceptions of God. To give an example, I'm not happy about the Buddha's contention that questions about the eternity of the world are not relevant to salvation.

C: Yet the contingency of the world is compatible with its eternity. St Thomas Aquinas, you may recall, asserted that the finitude of the world in time has to be taken on revelation, but cannot be proved by reason—and this despite the fact that he used the argument from the contingency of the world.

J: Yet I'm not sure how far this affects what I am claiming, namely that the act of creation is analogical history. All I was wanting to say was that there is a harmony of the kind I suggest between the notions of creation and historical revelation.

C: There is, too, another aspect of the matter which ought to be made plain. There's a strong strand of feeling in Hinduism, as I understand it, to the effect that the cycles of creation and destruction of successive universes and the rhythm of cosmic events are a sort of sport on the part of God—a cosmic dance, for instance, performed out of sheer exuberance, and without ulterior motive. Is this too misleading?

H: No, for there is Śiva's dance, and the emphasis on the destructive as well as the creative powers of the Godhead. This often enough causes offence to Westerners, though I'm not sure why. Is not God a terrible Being? Isn't the fear of the Lord the beginning of wisdom?

J: Let's not dispute about the meaning of that.

C: At any rate, there is a rough contrast, such as I have been hinting at. It appears to me that the stress, in the Christian revelation, upon the creation as a sheer act of will by God chimes in with our sense of the *purpose* of history. We often think of an act of will as being deliberate, and as having a purpose beyond itself. We do things *in order that* some purpose may be fulfilled. On the other hand, the notion of emanation or of the self-evolution of the Divine Being doesn't seem to have this same atmosphere of purpose, ulterior purpose. Even where, for instance in the *Upaniṣads*, this evolution is traced to the desire of the Divine Being, there does not seem to be so much idea of purpose as in the Christian picture. When it is said about the First Being: 'He desired, Let me be many; let me be born', one does not have the same flavour of contingency! It's hard to put these things very precisely, since there are so many shades and depths of meaning in any given revelation. Perhaps we can put the whole matter in another light by saying that our more *personal* picture of God implies the picture of a Being who acts; and in so far as Hinduism often gets away from, or goes beyond, this personalism, it tends to leave on one side the idea of purposive creation: the universe is a cosmic dance, a sport or game—and dancing and playing are things we do for their own sake, out of exuberance, and not for some special and further

purpose (centrally this is so, though of course there is pro-
fessionalism and there are those who take up sport to keep their
weight down!).

H: At this point, I'm willing to agree with J's contention
that all this does connect with our views of God. In so far as
many of us regard the personal picture of God as merely a
preliminary truth, we also regard creation by act of will or out
of desire as a preliminary myth. And further, our view of God
as 'beyond good and evil' harmonizes with mythological
descriptions of the destructiveness, as well as the creativity, of
God. And too—this is where we started—the cycle of *saṁsāra*
is in accord with the idea of a sportive, rather than purposive,
creation. You might have mentioned too how sportiveness goes
with the Advaitin thesis that the world is illusory, a colossal
conjuring-trick, almost a kind of entertainment. This cuts
against your 'realistic' view of history.

C: Yes, it has been remarked that Christianity is the most
'materialistic' of the world's religions, partly, of course, because
Christ by His incarnation sanctifies the material world. (If we
regard Communism as a Christian heresy, there is an interesting
application of this thought.) Another thing: J has emphasized
that the Creation is 'analogical history'. The same thing can
be said, perhaps, about the Fall.

CB: Analogical? I thought it was to be taken literally—or
perhaps I'm out of touch with modern exegesis. If I am, it's
because the Theory of Evolution and your increased knowledge
of pre-history have *made* you interpret Genesis allegorically!
One thing that can certainly be said by us old-fashioned people
of the East is this. Our belief in rebirth and in the immense
duration of the cosmos squares very much better with modern
science! We have always recognized our kinship with the
animals, since one can be reborn in animal form. Some of our
most delightful stories about the Buddha describe his earlier
lives in the forms of animals. Also, we don't have any trouble
over the time-scale of the universe as revealed in modern
science. We always knew it was staggering.

C: This I concede, and we've had to revise our ideas rather drastically. But the story of the Fall contains a profound truth, even if we can't confidently say that there was a man called Adam who . . .

CB: Do you mind my interrupting? I've just thought of a way in which rebirth is like Original Sin. Earlier you expressed intellectual difficulty over the doctrine of *karma*. And people have often found the Buddha's teaching about this particularly troublesome. For he described rebirth simply in terms of causation, as though there's no permanent something which goes from one birth to the next. This state causes that state, and so on, and when the body perishes, rebirth is simply the result of craving. In effect rebirth is just an extension of the flow of events, each causing the next to arise, which constitutes individual existence. Now people haven't understood how bad *karma* can be transmitted from one 'individual' to another if there is no permanent underlying something to carry it forward and to link the distant past with the distant future. I do not profess to explain this here. But it strikes me that the inheritance of sin may be just like this transfer of bad *karma*. And so, if you're going to accept your Christian teaching on the matter, I don't see why you find ours so difficult.

C: But isn't there a difference still? Ours is a hereditary communication of sin, while yours is not. If you like, what I find baffling is that you believe in a special connection between particular individuals, so that they have particular and different inheritances. On the other hand ours is a *general* doctrine and says something about human nature as such. Of course, if you wished to present your belief as pointing to the inextricable connection between members of society, past and present and future, and to the fact that we in some sense inherit evil tendencies, I would be with you. But surely you can't easily do this, since you believe in individual canalizations of *karma*.

CB: But at least we see that we're not quite so far off each other's viewpoint as was earlier suggested, and I think we see clearly now where the difference lies. It's worth repeating too that your notion of sin is definitely connected with the concept of God and isn't simply a matter of 'evil tendencies'. Also, of course, there are the animals. You Christians have in the last century or so come to see more clearly that we have certain duties to animals, that they should be treated more kindly than your tradition thought. But it's always been our belief that there is no sharp line between men and other living beings, and that all living beings should be treated with respect and compassion. And this is not unconnected, of course, with our belief in rebirth. This is a singular advantage of the latter.

H: Even that which is regarded often as a genial absurdity in Hinduism, the sacredness of the cow, points in the same direction.

J: But surely the animals were put into the world for men's use?

CB: But here you are appealing to a distinction which we do not recognize. We've always thought of the universe as of one piece. Indeed, the Jains go so far as to regard atoms as containing souls, and so they don't tread too violently upon the ground for fear of crushing them. This may be an extreme absurdity, but it is erring in the right direction. What we stress is that animals and men are kin.

C: Whereas we look on man as a special creation. This needn't be taken too literally, but at any rate it implies that men have souls, while animals do not. But I suppose that this is an unreal distinction in Buddhism, since for you *no one* has an eternal soul.

CB: You could say so. But men of course do have the capacity for salvation. We do certainly regard animal life as an inferior condition, and our legends about the Buddha's career do, of course, end up with his being reborn in human form. So in this respect our respective beliefs begin to coalesce. The normal condition of *nirvāṇa* is humanity. So if you simply want to translate 'having a soul' as 'being capable of salvation', then we are in agreement, more or less. But I do suggest that your concept carries with it a firm distinction between men and beasts which we do not make.

C: Still, one should guide one's moral judgments in accordance with the facts. And if we do not believe that my cat used to be somebody's aunt, it is pointless to treat her as though she were! Nevertheless I wouldn't deny that rebirth doctrine itself may be in part due to a moral perception which has often been lacking in Western culture.

M: Forgive my intrusion, but can we see where we've got to? I have been a bit bewildered by the twists and turns of this discussion.

C: If you'll let me assume the job of chairman again, I shall try to sum up our agreements and disagreements about rebirth and salvation. First, we have concurred in differing about rebirth itself. Second, we have seen that there need be no incompatibility between Eastern and Western views on what salvation is salvation *to*, even if there is a divergence about what it is salvation *from*. Of course, some doctrines, such as Advaita and Theravāda Buddhism, do *not* square with theism as they stand. But there are some theologians who, while accepting rebirth in the Hindu manner, nevertheless come close to our view of immortality. This shows, I think, the priority of doctrines about God. Third, we noted that rebirth accords well with a strong element in Hinduism and Buddhism—namely, the idea that liberation is a very *strenuous* business and therefore can be attained only by a small minority of those living at any one time. The ordinary person always has plenty of chances to come. Fourth, we saw that rebirth, with its hint of a cyclical universe, fits in better with one sort of doctrine of God, whereas the belief in a personal Creator of a contingent cosmos harmonizes with the 'historical' attitude to life and revelation. Fifth, we considered the way in which rebirth is more easily adaptable to certain findings in modern science, and lends itself to a compassionate attitude towards animals. Sixth, we saw that the Judaic religions make a distinction between men and animals which the belief in rebirth implicitly denies, though in practice if we think of the soul in terms of the capacity for salvation we find that there is no great gulf fixed between East and West. These, roughly, are our conclusions.

H: I was impressed by the way J brought out the connection between different views of the cosmos and different views of God. It would therefore seem unrealistic to tackle any further questions before we get to the heart of our disagreements about God. True, we've already considered polytheism and mono-theism or monistic pantheism, and have opted conditionally for the latter. But it is obvious that considerable divergences exist between theism and certain Hindu and Mahāyānist teachings, and these ought to be dealt with first.

CB: Before that even, there is the Theravādin plea: why *should* we believe in a Creator or Absolute at all? You may recall that this question is still on our agenda, and it's obviously prior to any further theological disputations. Can we discuss it now?

C: Clearly we must consider this question which is (from a religious person) rather startling. It would be nice if you could explain in what way it is that you Theravādins fail to believe in a Transcendent Being, for it sometimes seems to me as though *nirvāṇa* implies such a belief.

45

III

NIRVĀṆA AND MYSTICISM

CB: I'm certainly used to this kind of request, since my Western friends find it puzzling that Buddhism, though offering a method of salvation, should not involve belief in God. You said that sometimes it seems as if *nirvāṇa* implies the notion of a Transcendent Being. But let's be clear on this. According to the Theravāda, *nirvāṇa* is not to be identified with any such Being. For the normal sense which is attached to the phrase 'Transcendent Being' implies that it is the Ground or Source of the cosmos (or in more theistic terms, the Creator). Now not only did the Buddha deliberately refrain from speaking about the Ground or Creator of the world, but certainly *nirvāṇa* isn't spoken of as an underlying Reality of this sort in our Pāli canon. It's true that it is referred to as the Uncreated, Unbegotten, Immortal—and so on. And so the difference between this transcendent state and mundane states, between this condition of liberation and ordinary conditions, is rightly emphasized. If there were no such contrast, it's hard to see that *nirvāṇa* would genuinely count as release from the round of rebirth. But beyond this the Buddha does not, according to our tradition at least, proceed. It's not in accord with the categories of his thought that *nirvāṇa* should be described as a transcendent Substance or Thing or Being. And as to whether the saint or *arhat* who has attained *nirvāṇa* survives after death, the Buddha declared that it's neither correct to say that he does nor that he doesn't, nor indeed that he both does and doesn't, nor even that he neither does nor doesn't! Such is the comprehensiveness of the Buddha's fourfold negation—a kind of double agnosticism!

M: Unkind people, of course, might suspect that he was evading the issue.

46

CB: Somebody suggested this very thing to him. But the Enlightened One astutely replied that to ask whether the saint survives after final *nirvāṇa* is like asking whether a flame, when it goes out, goes North. The assertion has no clear meaning: a flame neither goes North nor in any other direction. Thus it's neither correct to say that it goes North nor that it doesn't . . . and so on.

C: This sounds at first like certain modern philosophers in the West, but I take it that the Buddha's prohibition of the question wasn't simply due to the fact that it had no clear meaning. Am I right? Why I ask is simply this: that we all recognize that we can't talk about transcendent Beings or conditions in the way we talk about what goes on in the ordinary world; and so there's a grave degree of unintelligibility about all our utterances about such matters. Yet we nevertheless persist in speaking. Hence it would seem that the Buddha had a special reason for not persisting.

CB: May I broaden the scope of my answer? Regarding the particular issue of survival after the attainment of *nirvāṇa*, there is much to be said. In the course of our discussion, we have already touched on the point that belief in survival may conduce to a craving for survival, and hence a lack of complete detachment. But more generally, the Buddha was deeply concerned to put first things first. He was profoundly moved by the ignorance and suffering in the world, and sought simply for a cure. Theories are all very well, but often the good doctor is the one with experience, who neglects debatable speculations in favour of what works in practice. Likewise the Enlightened One, our spiritual doctor, isn't worried about speculative truth. Worrying about the constitution of a possible transcendent world is often likely to divert men from really getting down to the business of curing themselves. The Buddha concentrates upon the treatment of our suffering. True, his teachings involve this much of theorizing, if you like to call it that. But it is a diagnosis of our ills. And having given the diagnosis, he then proceeds directly to the cure. And all we need to know about this cure is that it is possible, and that liberation from the painful cycle of rebirth can in fact occur. This, then, is one great reason for his 'agnosticism'. This is religion stripped to its bare essentials. Then also the Noble Eightfold Path does culminate in peace and insight, and this supreme attainment isn't easily put into words. Here *nirvāṇa* has its analogies with mysticism elsewhere. This is a second great reason for the Buddha's agnostic manner of speaking.

C: And yet, as you've already indicated, certain things *are* said about *nirvāṇa*. This is why I think of it as hinting at a doctrine of a Transcendent Being. Perhaps, after all, the realization of *nirvāṇa* is a way of experiencing God.

CB: You may, if you like, try to interpret it in that way, but it's not how *we* would describe it.

M: One would have to show good reasons for such an interpretation. Since Buddhist and theistic doctrines are so different, I am indeed puzzled by the claim that such a reconciliation can be effected.

C: I'm not saying that *doctrines* can be reconciled. I'm saying that perhaps, from the Christian—or, rather, the theistic—point of view it may be possible to interpret *nirvāṇa* in terms of a kind of vision of God. After all, we have to make some kind of distinction between experience and interpretation. For instance, I wouldn't deny that Muḥammad had some experience of God, though I would not always go along with his way of putting it into words. Similarly I suspect that the Buddhist can have something like a vision of God, but I do not subscribe to his description of it in terms of *nirvāṇa*. I believe too that it can be shown in what ways *nirvāṇa* is analogous to a mystical vision of God. If CB will be good enough to mention some of the characteristic epithets applied to this transcendent state, I will try to show how they can be suggestively interpreted in a theistic way.

CB: Before I do that, a question! Are you saying not merely that we're wrong in our interpretation, but also that a theistic interpretation is positively forced upon one? If so . . .

C: No, that would be to put it far too strongly. For in any case how can I *both* maintain my distinction between experience and interpretation *and* blithely assert that some particular interpretation is absolutely inescapable? It would be grossly implausible. Of course, the experiences must *suggest* one way of expressing them rather than another. For instance, there are some revelatory experiences which are numinous in character, as we've seen, and which hint that we are confronted by a mysterious and somehow personal Being. But one wouldn't wish to say that they imply any sort of detailed verbal description. And then, secondly, I don't for a moment think that the Buddha was just wrongheaded in giving the minimal description which he did. But I *do* suggest that if we are already theists we can see how *nirvāṇa* can plausibly, though not unavoidably, be given a theistic interpretation. There are important analogies between that which is said about God and that which is said about the Buddhist goal.

CB: You mean, looked at from your point of view?

C: Yes and no. Yes, because we theists wish to do justice to your profound Buddhist insights. For if it's true that we have revelations from a personal Deity, then we wish to connect these with the undoubted spiritual attainments accruing upon the Noble Eightfold Path. *Nirvāṇa* looks to me like a reflection of the unitive life of some of our Christian mystics. But on the other hand, no, I'm not just looking at it from my point of view. For the analogies are there to be seen, even if after seeing them one might deny that they're absolutely compelling. The similiarities are suggestive, but not absolutely compelling. Indeed, the considerable resemblances between certain forms of Mahāyāna belief and Christianity lead me to think that I'm not alone in seeing such analogies.

JB: I don't want to interrupt this particular section of the discussion, but I'd be grateful if we can later on consider how close these resemblances between Christianity and the Mahāyāna really are.

M: And why should we concentrate thus on resemblances

between *Christianity* and the Great Vehicle? After all, this discussion of *nirvāṇa* is supposed to be directed to seeing if it could plausibly (though not compellingly) be interpreted in a *theistic* sense. Christianity isn't the only form of theism—and I'm not sure if it's even typically theistic, since the doctrine of the Incarnation does *prima facie* cut across orthodox belief in one Lord.

C: Let us not quarrel about that issue yet. It is not merely that there are surprising similarities between Christianity and some Mahāyānist teachings, but also that the Mahāyāna contains its versions of the religion of devotion and grace (for example, the preaching of Hōnen in Japan), which are not unlike the 'straight' theism of Islam and Judaism.

CB: If you want me, then, to mention some characteristic epithets ascribed to *nirvāṇa*, I shall start with a suggestive one: it is called *amata* or 'deathless', and 'the immortal place'.

C: This is certainly reminiscent of the theistic belief in the eternity or immortality of God. And I suppose it is so for two reasons. First, because both in Buddhism and in theism there is an indication that there is a realm 'outside time' in some way. And second, because just as faith in God enables one to overcome fear, especially the fear of death, so too the attainment of *nirvāṇa* leaves one wishing neither for survival nor for extinction, and so here too the spectre of mortality is laid.

CB: You would doubtless then lay stress also on the fact that *nirvāṇa* is called *akutobhaya*, 'with nothing to fear from anywhere'. The attainment of peace leaves the saint utterly secure: there is no threat of suffering.

J: Forgive my flippancy for a moment: but don't *arhats* ever get toothache?

CB: Of course. But it leaves them without mental distress. The pangs of ordinary mortality cease to disturb them. Of course, we can't quite imagine what this is like, but that's because, regrettably, we aren't saints. *Nirvāṇa*, remember, is the Other Shore which we have not reached. It is a haven, a place of refuge, a place of safety.

C: We too speak of God as a refuge or rock. All this links up with deathlessness and timelessness.

CB: The timelessness of *nirvāṇa* does, however, have to be viewed (so I think) in the light of certain meditative practices in Buddhism. For instance, those which are described in that great handbook of mysticism, the *Visuddhimagga* or *Path of Purity*. We can't understand *nirvāṇa* except in the context of contemplation. In that book one finds, for instance, a delineation of the *jhānas* or stages of meditation, which, though they do not constitute by themselves the attainment of *nirvāṇa*, nevertheless play a central part in Buddhist spiritual accomplishment— as witness the fact that the Enlightened One himself is said to have gone through these stages at the time of his decease. It would perhaps be fruitless for me to describe these methods of meditation in any detail here, but suffice it to say that their object is to attain serenity and insight through detachment from the visible world. And detachment is achieved by concentrating upon some isolated object, such as a blue flower or a circle of clay, and thereby removing from one's consciousness all extraneous and worldly thoughts or images. And in the higher stages one attempts to conceive of nothingness (the blue flower even is banished), as though the material world just didn't exist. In short one rises quite beyond the sphere of perceptions. And if one succeeds in gaining this purity of consciousness one is in a sense beyond time. For time is perceived by us by reference to the succession of ordinary mental states and perceptual experiences. By going beyond ordinary perceptions, one goes beyond time. Do not Western mystics report a similar thing?

C: As when Vaughan said: 'I saw Eternity the other night' and Ruysbroeck said: 'His coming consists, outside all time, in an Eternal Now'. Certainly the higher contemplatives do seem somehow to break the bounds of time, or have them broken for them (if the theistic interpretation of the matter is correct).

Can't we say, then, that there is a loose analogy between what is said of the hidden God and what is said about *nirvāṇa*? Both, though perhaps in different ways, are timeless.

M: I'm not certain why you speak of 'different ways' here.

C: I am only meaning that perhaps the two concepts of 'timelessness' have different sources in experience. Whereas God, as hidden behind or beyond all phenomena, is thereby not to be described in terms of temporal predicates, and whereas it is the numinous experience that yields assurance that there is such a Being (so we think), in the mystical or contemplative quest one doesn't look outwards at the revealing world but inwards towards the depths of one's own soul, or whatever we should call it. And thus the things which are said about and on the basis of the numinous and mystical experiences respectively may well be somewhat different, even if analogies exist between the two ways of speaking. Maybe it is crude of me to make such a bald distinction between the numinous and the mystical. But unless we do distinguish in this way, I find it hard to make much sense of the doctrinal differences between Buddhism and the theistic faiths. The numinous experience suggests the presence of an unseen Power, before whom it is appropriate to bow down in worship. But the phenomenology of all this seems very different from that of the inner quest for peace and insight which we find in Buddhism and elsewhere. Certainly there are analogies between this peace and the peace of God, between this insight and the foretaste of the beatific vision which Christian contemplatives describe. But theistic mysticism is perhaps not mysticism in its pure or minimal form. For that, I turn to the Theravāda. Let me not be misunderstood. I'm not using the word 'pure' in an evaluative way. I'm not saying that the Buddhist interpretation of inner peace and the Buddhist techniques of contemplation are correct, though I admire them very much. I'm simply saying that in the Theravāda we have a *minimal* interpretation. For whereas among Muslims and Christians, for example, the inner vision is definitely and clearly interpreted in terms of God—God whom we learn of principally in another way, in the context of worship—the Theravāda does not introduce this extra content into their descriptions. It fails to connect up (whether rightly or wrongly), inner insight with the object of worship. In this sense it is a purely mystical religion, at core. And thus although I wish to point to the analogies between *nirvāṇa* and the Divine Being which would at least make plausible an identification of the mystical goal with the object of worship, nevertheless I think it is necessary, in order to make the situation intelligible, to distinguish rather sharply at first between the two strands of religious experience. In this way we can understand roughly how it is that you can have on the one hand a religion which concentrates exclusively upon the worship of a Divine Being (I'm thinking of certain phases of Judaism and Islam) and, on the other hand, as in the Theravāda, a religion where worship has no central part to play. Thus, to return to the discussion of timelessness, I suspect that there are differences between the concepts of eternity relating respectively to that which is discovered in mystical and numinous experience. Nevertheless, as we've seen, similarities exist; and seeing that the use of words like 'outside time' is not fixed by the possibility of a literal application of them (our speech about the transcendent realm being analogical), it may be quite legitimate to press these similarities. Similar remarks apply to other analogies between *nirvāṇa* and God. Can we, then, go on?

CB: Well, another common epithet applied to *nirvāṇa* is *nicca* or 'permanent'. This is, of course, by contrast with everything in the world, for all things, says the Buddha, are impermanent. *Nirvāṇa* is not included in this flow of evanescent causes and effects.

C: So, then, its permanence is a kind of changelessness, and this is in line with what we say about God. It's true that theists do not usually assert that the things in the world are impermanent in precisely your sense. And as was pointed out earlier, Christianity is pretty 'materialistic' and affirms the full reality of the cosmos. But we certainly do draw a contrast between the realm of the mutable and the realm of the changeless, between the finite and the infinite.

53

CB: The Theravāda, by the way, doesn't say that things are *unreal*, merely that they are *impermanent*: we do not agree with Śaṅkara, that the world is illusory. This, perhaps, is partly because morality (which the Buddha emphasized so much as part of the Eightfold Path) becomes meaningless.

H: Well, not entirely. From the standpoint of the highest truth, ordinary duties lose their significance, but in the sphere of lower truth (where we all start) they are part of the whole duty of man. But let's not go into this topic now, for we shall have an opportunity to discuss the Advaita Vedānta later.

C: Despite the realism of the Theravāda, doubtless connected as you say, CB, with the richness of moral insight displayed in the Buddha's teachings, nevertheless the impermanence of things constitutes a defect, so to speak. Not only the suffering implicit in worldly things, but also their impermanence, points to the contrasted abiding peace which, on your view, only *nirvāṇa* can give. Thus I think it would be legitimate to compare the theistic description of God with the 'immutability' of *nirvāṇa*.

CB: Yes, but note again that there isn't a relation of *dependence* between the impermanent and the permanent. Or at least the Buddha was silent about this: we do not want to commit ourselves in this to extraneous speculations.

C: Nevertheless, *nirvāṇa* is in some sense transcendent, is it not?

CB: Yes, for it does involve going beyond ordinary existence: one reaches the Other Shore. In terms of meditation, one reaches the sphere of neither-perception-nor-non-perception—something like a state of pure consciousness: and this is to go beyond the ordinary experience which, so to speak, constitutes our world. But one does have to be careful about what one means by 'transcendence'. J aptly pointed out how this notion is, in the theistic context, inseparable from God's holiness. But our Buddhist picture of transcendence is different. I mean this: that the Buddha spoke of *nirvāṇa* as though it lies outside the ordinary stream of impermanent events: and one can gain release by freeing oneself from the causal sequence determined by craving. It's not that *nirvāṇa* lies *behind* the world's events; rather it is the possibility of freeing oneself from them. Moreover, *nirvāṇa* isn't exactly one substance, like a sea, which different people *enter*: each person attains his *own nirvāṇa* (except in so far as the notion of separate individuality already disappears here). So there are certainly different shades of meaning in the two concepts of transcendence.

C: Which brings us back to my initial claim: that there is a loose resemblance which, though it doesn't entail a theistic interpretation, at least helps towards making it plausible. We can't put it more strongly than that.

CB: And provided you don't put it more strongly, I won't contest it (even though I feel no strong impulse to believe in theism).

C: Another thing about *nirvāṇa*. It has always struck me that those who attain it in this life are described as gaining a kind of bliss which is reflected in the serenity of their behaviour, and as acquiring a depth and power of character which is quite extraordinary. It is understandable that I, as a theist, can't help thinking of this in terms of the grace and power which God confers. For those who believe in one Holy Being surely wish to ascribe to Him all power and holiness, and thus we believe that spiritual joys and strengths come from Him. The holiness of man where it (all too rarely) exists is the reflected holiness of God.

CB: Though again we must be careful. The bliss which you mention, though it fits in with the glowing description of the beauty of *nirvāṇa*, cannot be compared perfectly. For if one were to delight in it, it wouldn't be the true Buddhist serenity. One mustn't become attached even to this! But perhaps in some sense it would be all right to describe *nirvāṇa* as blissful.

C: Certainly, for the peace of God passes all understanding.

H: As I see it, you two have reached a rough agreement that

55

there is some sort of resemblance between the conceptions of God and of *nirvāṇa*, since the former includes deathlessness, immutability, a kind of transcendence and supreme value, together with the highest kind (somehow) of blissfulness. And indeed I'm grateful for this discussion, for it certainly tends towards confirming our famous Brahman-Ātman doctrine, that the Self and God are somehow one. For is not the realization of the Self close to Buddhist *nirvāṇa*?

J: Perhaps there's been too much sweetness and light, if I may be pardoned for saying so. I'd like to hear a bit more about your disagreements. It's all very well to show that there are loose resemblances between certain Buddhist and theistic assertions, but after all we began by stressing the fact that Theravāda Buddhism has nothing much in common with the religion of worship.

CB: Perhaps I was being too easy-going. But that, you must recognize, is a Buddhist characteristic! If an Englishman were to ask me what he ought to do to gain salvation, I'd be inclined to say to him: 'Become a better Christian!' We recognize that there may be different paths to salvation, and each man must 'work out his own salvation with diligence'. Yet of course we Theravādins see full well that our doctrines are not theistic: in that connection, we are agnostic. So if you say to me, 'What are the differences between us and the theists?' I can tell you at once. *Nirvāṇa* isn't a substantive Being underlying the cosmos, it doesn't make sense to call it Creator, one does not worship it or even the Buddha, we don't pray to it (a meaningless suggestion) or even to the Buddha—and so on. These are surely differences enough!

C: Yet I suppose that if you were to believe in a Creator you would connect *nirvāṇa* explicitly with Him? Perhaps you would do what some of our Hindu friends have done, and call *nirvāṇa*, in a literal manner, 'becoming God'. So that the important issue remains, as to why you Theravādins reject the religion of worship and sacrifice. Was it simply because the Buddha was unhappy about the religious practices in his day?

Was it that the religion of the Vedas simply did not commend itself to him? Or is there a deeper reason?

CB: There are certainly plenty of indications in our scriptural tradition that the Buddha *was* dissatisfied with the Brahmins' religion. But perhaps there still remains the deeper reason you ask about. For who has seen God? And how can He be the Creator of such a suffering world? Isn't it better to get down to the solid business of curing the evils of the world, rather than hazarding theories about the next world?

C: Yet, though no man has seen God (in so far as He is invisible), we have believed that there are revelations or intimations of the Divine Being. And the problem of evil is not insuperable.

CB: But you've already remarked that the resemblances in virtue of which you link mystical insight with the object of worship are loose. If they are loose, and if a link be necessary, then your doctrines become both hazardous and complicated.

C: I'm not denying that. Certainly, if we take the mystics seriously, we must recognize that there are different ways to God, and these have to be integrated, even if tensions still remain. For instance, I suppose that the Brahman-Ātman doctrine is a way of bringing together the religion of sacrifice on the one hand with the inner contemplative quest towards insight and knowledge on the other. And certainly the identification of the Self with Brahman, the Power pervading and sustaining the cosmos, presents its difficulties, as also the Ṣūfī teachings created tensions within Islam. Assuredly it is a little surprising that the great God who rules the cosmos can be found within the heart 'tinier than a mustard-seed', as the *Upaniṣad* says. And it's difficult sometimes to resist the impression that the mystics' tendency to speak of deification is unorthodox and even perhaps blasphemous. All this I grant. But if one believes in a personal God it is hard not to allow that there is a way to Him through mysticism, through contemplation. This may lead to complications of doctrine, absurdities, difficulties; but the result is a marvellous welding together of the insights of different types of religious practice. And history may be on my side in these remarks. For, on my reading of the situation, early Islam was understood in its early days simply as a religion of worship of and obedience to Allah, and yet it flowered also, through the Ṣūfīs, into a faith where the profound and beautiful interior visions were also seen as a kind of contact with God. Then, conversely, isn't it significant that Buddhism itself became proliferated, in the Mahāyāna, in such a way that the intuitions of the numinous were given a central place? All the richness of the Great Vehicle perhaps outweighs its complications. The Theravāda is wonderfully simple and austere in its main insight, but was it always meant to stay thus?

CB: You seem to want to have it both ways! You recommend monotheism (in distinction from polytheism) for its simplicity, but now you say you want richness even if this implies complication!

C: Simplicity isn't the *only* point in favour of monotheism. We shouldn't insist so strongly on simplicity that a central part of religion, the intuitions and revelations of the numinous, is excluded.

CB: But these *aren't* entirely neglected in our religion. We don't object to ceremonies (such as those concerned with the Sacred Tooth at Kandy) which satisfy the ordinary layman's desire to venerate something greater than himself.

C: Yet these intimations of the numinous are given no *doctrinal* application? What may seem to the ordinary man a ritual of worship is explained by you simply as a means of expressing reverence for the great (human) Teacher and for his Law. Perhaps you are right, and yet . . .

CB: But look at it from your point of view: you already grant that the mystical quest is a way to the Truth. And so we aren't cut off from that Truth. Why object if we stick to what is certain and assured and neglect that which is doubtful and speculative?

C: Our objection would, I think, be this: that although the

simplicity of your doctrines is wonderful, nevertheless the truth may be richer than this. If you like, you buy simplicity at the expense of denying yourself this richness. It is a hard business balancing the merits of our respective approaches! But then we get back to rebirth. Maybe you're right and that your Noble Eightfold Path is definitely a way to the Truth, but it is a tough way, and for us who don't believe in rebirth it seems strange and hard that the opportunity to see the Truth is for the very few rather than for the many.

J: But it may be a hard world; and can you argue that what is undesirable from your point of view is therefore false?

C: Yes, you are right. But if a good God exists, then . . .

CB: But here you're appealing to your own presuppositions.

C: Well, all that I can say is that I can't neglect the experience of men like Moses, Job, Muhammad, St Paul and many others. I find it hard to reject the testimony of so many ordinary and extraordinary men and the corporate witness of the Church. Nor do I find it easy to doubt my own intimations of God.

CB: I don't want you to *reject* them. But I say merely that our reverent agnosticism gives you the essential truth, and beyond it one doesn't *need* to go.

M: You've not after all had the inestimable benefit of really listening to our Prophets. The unmistakeable power of their revelations is not to be neglected.

C: And at this point we have to agree to differ with CB. We have seen that a theistic interpretation of *nirvāṇa* is not impossible; but one would find it plausible only if one already takes seriously the religion of worship and the revelations of the numinous associated therewith. These latter, we hold, confirm our belief in a personal Being.

CB: And we, for our part, can stress the simplicity and minimal nature of our beliefs. This may well commend Buddhism to those who are having intellectual difficulties over belief in God (and perhaps you'd rather have a man an incipient Buddhist than an atheist!). But no Buddhist would condemn theistic beliefs out of hand: our attitude is one of tolerance and (I hope in more senses than one) enlightenment. Perhaps this is already obvious from the remarkable range of beliefs, which Westerners find so baffling, which we allow within the Buddhist fold. We have indeed, succeeded in being a missionary religion without dogmatism. Thus fine is the Buddha's gentle and compassionate example.

C: Yes, that is one of the greatest achievements of Buddhism, this preaching of peace and gentleness. Yet we're all equally men, and sinful, and though there have been religious wars and persecutions in the history of Christianity, this is partly due, not to our moral inferiority as compared with the (on the whole) peaceful Buddhists, but because our religion is necessarily explosive and urgent. As J said earlier, we have before us the burning vision of the one Lord. Is it any wonder that the wickedness of men should turn this explosive quality of the religion of the living God into the wrong channels? However, we're getting off the main point, and perhaps this is because we have exhausted this topic. We have agreed where the theist has to disagree with the Theravādin, and have seen the reasons why. Would it be appropriate to turn to consider that which at some points comes close to Buddhism, namely Śaṅkara's non-dualism? It is, among educated people at least, a very influential form of Hindu belief. Perhaps you would care to say something about it, H?

IV

THE WORSHIP OF GOD

H: Just as there is a wide range of beliefs allowed within the Buddhist fold, so too in Hinduism: so perhaps the credit shouldn't just go to the Buddha and his disciples, but to the spirit of Indian religion! Now although non-dualism—the Advaita Vedānta—is only one of our schools of theology, and although its doctrines aren't in fact held widely by Hindus, it's still a most influential form of Hinduism. It has also made its converts in the West. Its chief interest for us in the present discussion is that whereas we can find beside it within Hinduism doctrines which are not unlike the Theravāda (I'm referring to agnostic Sāṅkhya) and those which approximate to theism (as among the *bhakti* theologians), the Advaita represents in beautifully compact form a midpoint between these systems. Moreover, it interprets the teachings of the *Upaniṣads* in a wonderfully systematic way.

M: But it's not the only interpretation?

H: No. For the different schools of philosophy (or theology, if you prefer the word) interpret them differently. But perhaps no single interpretation can do justice to the richness and diversity of insights contained in those writings. However, one can't help admiring the amazing job which Śaṅkara did in organizing those insights, even though we may differ from him.

C: What do you take to be the crucial point of interpretation of those scriptures in Śaṅkara?

H: Undoubtedly it's his way of construing the famous *Tat tvam asi* in the *Chāndogya Upaniṣad*, the 'great saying' as it is called, when it is asserted 'That art thou'.

M: Meaning?

H: Meaning, according to Śaṅkara, that 'That', i.e. Brahman, is identical with 'Thou', i.e. the Self. It is said also: 'Brahman is Ātman'. In other words, the Power which sustains the cosmos is numerically identical with that immortal element residing within each one of us. You'll remember that according to our scriptures Brahman is the Reality of reality—it is the one truly real Being. And Śaṅkara took this principle to its conclusion, by affirming that all else is unreal. By the same token, there are not individual souls. Each man's Self is the one great Self. Brahman-Ātman is the sole reality.

J: But one certainly has to explain the existence of the *apparent* world!

H: Which Śaṅkara certainly undertook to do. One can look at the matter from two seemingly different points of view, from the side of Brahman or from the side of the Self. Looked at in the former way, the world is *māyā* or illusion, and is produced by the creative Lord in his capacity as the cosmic illusionist. Not that Śaṅkara denies empirical validity to ordinary knowledge; but from the standpoint of higher truth the world is illusion. Or looking at the matter from the side of the Self, the world is the product of *avidyā* or ignorance. This leads us to a most interesting point in Śaṅkara's system—his distinction between higher and lower knowledge. It's not just a distinction between spiritual and empirical knowledge, but it cuts through religious doctrines. In higher truth Brahman is without attributes, save those of Being, Consciousness and Bliss; in lower truth, It appears as the *Īśvara* or Lord, who is all-knowing, almighty, providential, who creates, maintains and dissolves the universe, who pervades it in His capacity as Inner Ruler. What better description could you have of the theistic ideas of divine transcendence and immanence? Yet all this is part of the lower knowledge. And so our belief in such a Being is itself a kind of ignorance: just a preliminary picture.

C: In some ways Śaṅkara's system is like Eckhart's; I remember that the comparison is made in Otto's great book *Mysticism East and West*. But how can we be expected to concur with Śaṅkara in allowing that the picture of God as a personal Being is merely the lower truth?

H: But certainly Śaṅkara makes a place for orthodox theism. He doesn't leave it on one side, as does the Theravādin.

M: But the thing is upside down! Why make theism the lower, rather than the higher, truth?

H: You see, we don't want to anthropomorphize God. What Śaṅkara does is to describe Brahman Itself in such a way that attributes arising from some *relationship* do not, in highest truth, apply to It. I mean, for example, that to call God Creator cannot be the highest truth, since creation is not an absolute necessity. Put it another way. God is something else before there is ever a creation; and we call Him Creator looking merely from the standpoint of the world. Similarly there are what you call revelations of God to men, but these are not part of His essential nature. The only attributes which truly express God's inner nature are those of Being, Consciousness and Bliss.

J: But the first of these is, though apt, somewhat empty. The term 'Being' does not *describe* that Being in any way, does it?

H: Perhaps that's an advantage, if we wish to avoid anthropomorphism.

M: But this strong desire to avoid anthropomorphism is most paradoxical, coming from you. For the reason why we Muslims wish to avoid thinking of Allah as a sort of super-man is simply because this would be blasphemous. If we're to express the true majesty of God one must go beyond the literal meanings of God's attributes. But our wish to avoid blasphemy comes from our overwhelming concern to *worship* God. Now isn't it paradoxical that you should recommend Śaṅkara's system as successfully avoiding anthropomorphism when worship is only regarded there as of secondary significance?

H: Perhaps the lesson of this is that worship has a kind of inner logic which leads it to transcend and supersede itself. But

I agree that it wouldn't be right to defend Śaṅkara's system *simply* on the ground that it avoids anthropomorphism.

C: J asked about the concept *Being*, and I'm reminded of ways in which some of our Christian mystics talk about Being. Ruysbroeck, for instance, somewhere talks of a 'meeting and dying into the nudity of Pure Being' and Boehme of seeing the 'Being of all Beings'. Is it a coincidence, or is there some reason why mystics speak often in these ontological terms? What I am trying to get at is this: that Śaṅkara, in stressing Consciousness and Bliss, is stressing those very qualities which appear in the purified soul and which are consonant with the inner mystical vision. For isn't it the goal of the Advaitin mystic to realize a purity of consciousness and a supreme bliss? I'm therefore suggesting that the odd one out among these three attributes, that of Being, is also in some intimate way appropriate to what is found in interior experience, as Ruysbroeck and Boehme seem to testify. But I speak, perhaps, in riddles.

CB: You are, I think, getting at something which we touched on earlier, that purity of consciousness involves clearing it of all the perceptions and images which are normally and constantly found in it. And so there's nothing left to *describe*— or at least there's nothing left to describe in ordinary language. And so the word 'Being', by virtue of its voidness of descriptive content, is eminently suitable. But if so, I find it difficult to understand why the Buddha didn't speak in the same way of *nirvāṇa*, as Pure Being. But I suppose that at least a part of the explanation is that through his doctrine of *anattā*, or non-self, which denies the existence of an eternal spirit underlying either the world or psychological phenomena, he was attempting to rid men of the delusive interest in immortality. And he saw, very perspicaciously, that questions about the origin of the cosmos are liable to issue in unedifying disputation—an intellectual substitute for the hard work of treading the Noble Eightfold Path. And so as a consequence he didn't wish to speak of *nirvāṇa* as the merging into some Being, nor did he wish to speak of an underlying Reality. Rather, with lucid economy of preaching, he confined himself to the essential contrast between the ordinary impermanent states of existence and the state of liberation.

JB: I'm not altogether happy with your interpretation of the Buddha's silences, since we Mahāyānists contend that his preaching at that time was merely the first stage of a developing revelation, well adapted to the condition of men then. But I'm interested in the suggestion that the word 'Being' gains its aptness from its descriptive emptiness. This reminds me inevitably of the central conception of a very famous Mahāyānist philosophical school, namely the conception of *Śūnyatā* or Voidness. This was given a wide application: but perhaps again it is in consonance with mystical experience and the Cloud of Unknowing that we should speak of the Absolute as Void, *Śūnya*. However, we'll doubtless have an opportunity of discussing this later.

H: But surely the word 'Being' isn't used *simply* because of its adaptable descriptive emptiness? Why not use no words at all?

JB: Remember that you sometimes have to use words to show what words won't do!

H: Even so, I'm still dissatisfied. True, I recognize that also words like 'Being' and 'Reality' signify something of a *value-*judgment. For to speak of something as a *real* such-and-such is often to commend it, and we certainly think of the highest Reality as somehow of the highest value. But surely we also want to say that the Being really *is*, and this is partly why we use the term 'Being'.

C: Yes, this is surely part of our meaning. But I was emphasizing the descriptive emptiness in order to show how this concept links up with mystical experience, that's all.

H: What you're suggesting is that it is through mystical insight, the realization of the Ātman as we call it, that we come to see the truth of Śaṅkara's characterization of Brahman.

C: Yes. Or rather no, for I don't say that *we* do. I for one have neither the virtue nor the grace to be blessed with such an interior vision. I merely go by the reports of the spiritual geniuses whose work I've read. Nevertheless, though I recognize that the concepts of Being, Consciousness and Bliss have a connection with inner knowledge, it would be far from my thoughts to accept the simple identification of the soul and God which we seem to find in Śaṅkara.

H: Perhaps it depends what we mean by 'soul'. It's sometimes used by you Westerners to mean, simply, consciousness— the ordinary flow of experiences, united in some way. Now Śaṅkara makes a clear distinction between the real Self and the empirical selves with which we're normally acquainted. If then by 'soul' you're referring to the empirical self, then quite obviously Śaṅkara's *not* saying that the soul and God are one. The empirical self is part of the grand illusion. When he says that 'Brahman is Ātman' he's not saying that the empirical self is Brahman.

C: I grant the distinction. But in any case I wasn't meaning the empirical self, even though I hold that what you would call the Ātman is connected in some, quite intimate, way with the empirical self. No, I was meaning what some have called the ground of the soul, or the spark or the apex of the soul. I refer to that basic element in consciousness which can become pure in the experience of contemplatives. Now it's perhaps natural sometimes for such contemplatives to identify that apex with Being itself, with God Himself. For, as we often have remarked, there is in this state seemingly (and I say seemingly) no distinction between subject and object. For it's from the situation of observation, where a person sees something which he recognizes to be distinct from himself, that we draw this conception of two different entities, the subject and the object. And therefore, when there's no such observation, then it's natural to say that the seer and the seen are not distinct. But the theist cannot concur with any doctrine that men can in any sense be *identified* with God, that they can in effect *become* God. However natural this manner of speaking may be, for such reasons as I've mentioned, it can hardly be thought, by the theist, that the great gulf between man and God can be bridged in *this* way. As Devendranath Tagore said: 'What we want is to worship God; if the worshipper and the object of worship are one, how can there be any worship?' And despite what I've said about the descriptive emptiness of the word 'Being' and analogously of the mystical state, it's hard to suppose that the so-called 'interior' vision really has no content. And if it has a content perhaps it's appropriate to speak, but in a highly circumspect manner, of a difference between that which is seen and the one who sees. Maybe there is an *analogical* distinction between subject and object. Perhaps this is what some mystics are getting at when they speak of 'Spiritual Marriage'. And perhaps too this is the root of the comparison in the *Upaniṣads* between the mystical state and being in the arms of one's dear wife. Here is adumbrated a 'two who become one': a distinction of subject and object which is yet a unity. These may be vague and unsatisfactory uses of language, but here one's bound to go beyond the usual limits of language.

M: And there's a further criticism of Śaṅkara which the theist may wish to make. For by his sheer non-dualism, by his contending that the Brahman-Ātman is 'one without a second', Śaṅkara necessarily denies the difference between individual souls (in this deeper sense of 'soul'). From the standpoint of lower knowledge, it's true, there are distinctions of individuals. But ultimately, there's no such distinction, on his system. It is indeed strange to say that we are all in essence the same Self.

H: But I don't think that you and C are putting enough emphasis on this lower knowledge in Śaṅkara. It's true that at first sight the doctrine of *māyā* is rather startling and suggests that Śaṅkara has lost touch with reality. And it's true that at first sight his abolute monism seems to deny human individuality. But he criticized the Buddhist doctrine of the Void (*Śūnyatā*) precisely because of its unrealism. He doesn't want to deny the existence of the Grand Illusion! It's merely that he characterizes the phenomenal world in a certain way by calling it an illusion or conjuring-trick. Likewise, he recognizes full well the differences between individuals in the world. All that you're objecting to is that he consigns ordinary knowledge and theistic religion (as ordinarily understood) to the sphere of lower truth. But as I've said, we can't seriously suppose that the description of God by reference to His activity as Creator and so forth is the *inner* truth about Him. Does He not exist independently of His creation, on the theistic view? And again, though we can believe that the soul is immortal, is it easy to make sense of the idea of an independent existence of souls in a transcendent realm? How does one distinguish one soul from another when they have reached the utterly transcendent state? At least Śaṅkara's system has a wonderful comprehensiveness and simplicity. And as I said before, it is perhaps an expression of the way in which theism must transcend itself. It is sometimes alleged, for example, by modernist Muslims, that belief in the eternity of the Qu'rān is setting up another god beside Allah, and this is an illustration of the Muslim desire to have an absolutely pure monotheism. Well, Śaṅkara's system at least rigidly denies 'in highest truth' the existence of *anything* (whether eternal soul or anything else) apart from Brahman. How can you object?

C: You've defended Śaṅkara eloquently, and after your exposition I hardly know where to begin. But surely, even despite what you've said about Śaṅkara's recognition of the 'existence' of the illusory world, it's nevertheless true that a certain *picture* is inevitably presented by the conception of *māyā*. I seem to remember that there's a poem attributed to Śaṅkara which begins, 'Think truly this life is but a dream'— and this overwhelmingly is the feeling conveyed by his doctrines. Now I agree, despite what I said earlier about Christian 'materialism', that the religious person, by having his eyes fixed on a higher realm, must come to see the world as not possessing the highest reality. Thus far we must go along with Śaṅkara. But to speak of this life as a dream is to give the wrong picture.

H: Tell me clearly why!

C: All right. I'll try to sum up our convictions. Within the sphere of worship and the numinous we find that there is a gulf fixed between the object of worship and the worshipper. And this distinction is reflected necessarily in our view of creation. For we also have to see the cosmos itself (though utterly dependent for its existence upon God) as having its *separate life*, so to speak. If there is a distinction between creatures and Creator there is a distinction between creation and Creator. This is one of the reasons for our 'realism'. And note, too, that this autonomy which we have is a sign of God's overflowing goodness and love. A loving God is one who cherishes what he creates to the extent of allowing it independence.

M: If you're getting on to the doctrine of free will, I may not be entirely with you, for we believe, in consonance with Muḥammad's shattering emphasis on the majesty of God, that we are predestined.

C: Perhaps we can return to that. But I think you'll agree with what I said about the independent *reality* of the cosmos, even if its working are entirely controlled by God. I'm saying, then, that our picture of the situation—albeit only a picture— is of a *gap*. So we can't accept Śaṅkara's absolute monism, which seems to deny it.

H: It doesn't deny your picture of a gap at the level of lower knowledge. And if what you are saying merely expresses a picture, then why object because instead of saying 'just a picture' Śaṅkara says 'lower knowledge'?

C: Perhaps I'm being too easy-going in talking just about 'pictures'. I was doing so because first of all we know full well that our descriptions of God are indeed inadequate, and second because abstract-sounding doctrines nevertheless enshrine a way of looking at things. For example, *transcendence* is a conception which enshrines a way of looking at God as beyond or behind the screen of the cosmos. But I don't want to say that because our theistic picture is just a picture, it is not a *good* picture. And the experience of our prophets and saints indicates the existence of a personal Object of Worship. This latter is, in our view, the

Supreme Reality. But Śaṅkara's doctrine, though it accommodates our picture, does definitely assign it second place to something else. It's the system of priorities I object to. To put the matter in a definitely Christian context, if God reveals Himself in Christ then He is in the fullest sense a Person, and I don't see that this truth is properly brought out by Śaṅkara.

H: But you wouldn't believe in the Incarnation unless you already had the idea that God is fully personal! So you can't appeal to the Incarnation to back your view of God. Belief in Christ *depends* on that view of God.

C: Yes, belief in the Incarnation does, as you say, presuppose something about God. But it also throws light on the nature of God. However, I apologize for bringing that in at the moment. We were discussing theism as such, and I guess I was confusing the issue by mentioning the Incarnation. It's hard to keep one's mind compartmentalized in these matters. Still, my point definitely remains, that we theists object to Śaṅkara's system of priorities, with its suggestion not merely that the religion of devotion and worship is somehow secondary, but also that the creation is not properly real.

H: But if pictures of God *are* just pictures, you surely will admit that there is a 'higher truth' beyond the pictures?

C: Yes, God, though a Person, is more than that. But though I recognize the existence of a 'higher truth', as you call it, I'm not tied to any particular formulation of that higher truth in terms of Being, Consciousness and Bliss. Nor do I wish to make a sharp divide between the higher and the lower truth. The picture of God as a personal Creator isn't something which we discard when we try to penetrate deeper into the mystery, but it's something which we progressively *enrich*. And where enrichment ceases we are left, not with doctrines, but with the Ineffable.

J: There's one point which has been worrying me in this discussion. You, C, have been stressing that Śaṅkara's characterization of the *nirguṇam* Brahman, the Brahman without attributes, is somehow impersonal. I'm not quite clear as to whether it really is: for I gather that *cit* or Consciousness is ascribed to Brahman, and this seems another way of saying that Brahman is in some way a person.

C: Perhaps so. But recall that this Brahman is not He but It. What corresponds to our idea of God is definitely the *Īśvara*, the lower manifestation of Brahman who rules and controls the cosmos. The higher Brahman is spoken of in less personal terms. I agree it's hard to do justice to the fine shades of meaning that different doctrines imply! Yet one is almost inevitably led to think of the higher Brahman as the *Absolute*—rather than as God.

H: Perhaps our discussion has so far been pretty inconclusive, but I think that it's becoming clear that there's not such a great divide between Śaṅkara's monism and theistic doctrine as was at first apparent. There are ways in which his view comes near to those of theists who stress the negative way and who wish to climb upwards beyond the orthodox descriptions of God. Yet there still seems to remain this disagreement about the independent reality of creatures. And even though I have urged that we should take Śaṅkara's lower truth seriously, this doesn't get over the fact that his rather sharp division of two levels of truth doesn't commend itself to theists.

C: Can I add something to that? Earlier we tentatively made a distinction between the religion of worship and the religion of mysticism or contemplation. And I think it was agreed that, in the nature of the case, there are certain impersonalistic tendencies in mysticism, since the interior vision transcends the world in which 'personality' is given its meaning. It is easy for mystics to mistake their goal in this way; or rather it is easy for us to misinterpret their words—for they are always struggling to express that which is other-worldly. Now it seems to me that Śaṅkara's doctrine is in line with a strong emphasis on *gnosis*, on mystical *vidyā* or knowledge. This makes it understandable that Eckhart should come close to him in some ways. Now such an emphasis is liable to result in a denial of the distinction between subject and object, a tendency to speak of deification, a preference for ontological terminology. Now I do not precisely reject these ways of speaking. Who am I to criticize the testimony of men who reached such spiritual heights? Nevertheless, we should remain careful as to how we integrate their insights with those of theism. If truly they are gaining an inner vision of God, then it is a communion with a Person. Moreover, though some mystics have emphasized those things which I have mentioned, think also of those others who have spoken in a different way (as we saw), in terms of Love and Spiritual Marriage.

H: I'm afraid you're only repeating yourself! You're only saying again that mysticism ought to be interpreted in a theistic manner. You begin with theism and fit the inner vision into it. Śaṅkara, you hint, is working in the opposite direction. But why not? What's wrong with his way of doing it?

C: Perhaps once more we have come to an impasse. But it's not as though I simply appeal to our revelations. It does seem to me that theism can give us a profound and beautiful way of integrating the insights of prophets with those of contemplatives and combining the paths of devotional worship and mystical endeavour. But if you try to do it the other way round the main teachings of theism begin to disappear: devotion fades and the revelations wither. While theism can convincingly absorb and enrich the mystical path without detriment to the latter, the mystical path cannot absorb theistic belief without relegating it to second place.

M: I agree with that. For though Ṣūfīsm brought a marvellous new depth to our understanding of the Qu'rān, the movement was, as history shows, fraught with a considerable menace of unorthodoxy.

H: You do worry a lot about orthodoxy!

M: Only by a stern conservatism can we preserve the purity of God's revelation. However respected a person may be and whatever spiritual accomplishments he may appear to

72

possess, however subtle his philosophizing, he must stand before the judgment of the Word of God.

H: If only it were so clear as to what the Word of God is! But don't think that because I defend Śaṅkara I am unsympathetic to theism. If I were to name one of our scriptures as supremely valuable, I would name the *Bhagavadgītā*—not very originally, but originality is no great virtue in these matters. Yet it scarcely seems to me that Śaṅkara's wonderful synthesis is obviously wrong. Equally I recognize that our *bhakti* theologians agree with many of the points which you have made. But how do we tell, after all, which picture is correct? Ultimately, I expect that it's a matter of individual experience.

C: I would merely stand upon two points, which I've already made. First, I cannot ignore the revelations of a personal God who is object of worship. Second, I find that though the numinous can absorb and enrich the mystical, the converse does not apply. But I grant also the simplicity and comprehensiveness of Śaṅkara's system.

H: There's a corollary to his doctrines which we ought to discuss briefly. You Western theists attribute men's spiritual ills to sin, but Śaṅkara looks upon them as due to ignorance. I certainly find this characteristically Indian view much more congenial and convincing.

C: So, in some moods, do I. But when confronted by the Holy One, how can we claim purity and holiness? The emphasis on sin is all bound up with our view of God. Where the highest aim is *vidyā* or knowledge, then obviously the contrasting defect will be a kind of ignorance. But our belief in the fact of sin is, partly at any rate, due to our exalted conception of God—or so we think. And although the story of the Fall may at times seem childish, it does attempt to explain the existence of sin and evil in the world. But that's a topic best left for the moment. We have already touched upon it, and are bound to come back to it when we come to discuss the nature of morality.

H: All we can say, then, by way of conclusion is that in regard to their doctrines of God the Advaita and theism differ considerably in *emphasis*, and that there is a corresponding difference in views about the cosmos and about man. But I suppose that one can reconcile the doctrines to some extent. After all, despite your strictures on the somewhat impersonal atmosphere of the attributes Being, Consciousness and Bliss, I think that your Christian theologians have applied analogues of these to the Godhead. Maybe one could work out some sort of rough correspondence to the Trinity doctrine (though Śaṅkara does not allow for an Incarnation).

JB: Since you mention the Trinity, it might be useful to discuss the Mahāyānist Three-Body doctrine; at first sight it bears, as you know, a remarkable resemblance to Christian belief. Some of the issues which you've been discussing will arise again there.

V

BUDDHISM AND THE TRINITY

C: Perhaps you could explain briefly how you understand your Three-Body doctrine.

JB: It may perhaps seem rather complicated, but so, to my mind, is Christian theology! According to the Three-Body doctrine or *Trikāya*, a Buddha can be considered as having three bodies (or aspects, if you like). First of all a Buddha has his *nirmāṇakāya* or 'transformation-body', and this is the guise in which he appears on earth, as in the case of the historical Buddha Gautama. And then there is the *sambhogakāya* or 'bliss-body', in which Buddha appears in celestial form. (There are, for instance, theophanies of this sort, where a Buddha appears to companies of *arhats* or Bodhisattvas.) Finally, all Buddhas are united in their *dharmakāya*, which is sometimes called the Absolute. This is the Ultimate Reality behind or within all phenomena (our philosophical schools sometimes dispute over how to characterize these matters). It is also said this Absolute and *nirvāṇa* are one and the same. You can see why this should be so, for if the state of release is Buddhahood, and if Buddhahood is at bottom just the Absolute, then *nirvāṇa* and the Absolute are one and the same.

M: I'm not sure why anyone should assert this complex set of peculiar doctrines. Could you give some enlightenment on this?

JB: Perhaps your request is too hard to fulfil. When we are dealing with that which is, in a sense at least, revealed doctrine, it is presumptuous to give reasons which would cover everything that is said. (Perhaps you will sympathize with my feeling that hitherto in this discussion, admirable as it has been, there has been too much eagerness to try to make everything in religious doctrine absolutely clear.) But I suppose that I can say something which will throw a little light on these doctrines. Of course, they go well beyond those of the Theravāda. For one thing, we criticize the Lesser Vehicle Buddhism for its exclusive adherence to the ideal of *arhat*-ship. We find difficulty in believing that this ideal leads to the moral and deeply compassionate attitude which so luminously was exhibited by the Buddha. It may seem to be working out your *own* salvation with diligence; but may it not lead to that very self-centredness which the Enlightened One himself so obviously condemned, and which, as we've seen, is one great reason for the Buddha's teaching that there is no self? On our view, the revelation goes beyond those economical teachings which Gautama, to wean men away from their lustful ignorance, is reported to have given. In short, there's a wider ideal which the ideal of *arhat*-ship prepares us for. This is the great vision enshrined in the concept of the Bodhisattva, the great being who is destined for Buddhahood. Here is seen the tremendous idea of Buddhist compassion in its greatest glory. For the Buddha-to-be, sorrowful at the suffering and ignorance of ordinary humanity (and for that matter animality), puts off his own *nirvāṇa* to work for the salvation of mankind. Out of the treasure-house of his merit, acquired in his arduous career towards final Enlightenment, he bestows upon others a sufficiency of merit for their assurance of ultimate salvation.

C: This is somewhat like our doctrine of grace.

JB: Yes, and it leads me to the first main point which I wish to make regarding the Three-Body doctrine—that in the ideal of the Bodhisattva we find intimations of the religion of devotion and worship so dear to the hearts of theists. The notion of celestial Buddhas, who preach such a doctrine of salvation, reminds us at first, I suppose, of the Gods. It's not for me to say whether or not our proliferation of celestial Buddhas looks like polytheism to alien eyes. I trust not! In its way this belief in the *sambhogakāya* does represent, at the level of phenomenal existence, those 'intimations of the numinous' about which we spoke earlier. And it is a comforting belief; for do we not hear, at this level, of Buddhas by the power of thought creating worlds such as the Pure Land of the West where the conditions for attaining *nirvāṇa* are peculiarly favourable? Yet it's not the final truth. For the final truth is that all Buddhas are one in the Absolute (or in the Void, *Śūnya*).

C: You've said quite a lot about the bliss-body; but what about the transformation-body? This is what especially concerns me, as it has analogies with the Christian doctrine of the Incarnation.

JB: I'm not sure how much you would approve of this belief, for you can see from the very word 'transformation' that there is a suggestion of magical power here.

H: *Māyā!*

JB: Yes, there are signs of *māyā* in our view, even if Śaṅkara may not have approved of the doctrine of *Śūnyatā*. As for the *nirmāṇakāya*, I confess to a certain docetism in our approach. There are many Buddhas who appear on earth (of course the Theravādins believe this too). Not for us the uniqueness of Incarnation! And clearly, many manifestations of the one underlying person or reality are quite naturally looked upon as appearances. And what harm is there in that? More philosophically, I would add that the metaphysical basis of the Mahāyānist doctrine of an Absolute is idealist, in a measure at least. Thus the Yogācārins and the Śūnyavādins both in different ways emphasize the unreality or emptiness of the material world. And so this is a second motive for looking on the earthly Buddhas, as *appearances* of an underlying Something.

C: This certainly demarcates your view from orthodox Christianity, which sets its face against docetism.

H: Why throw around these 'isms'? Is it so terrible to be a docetist? Is it so terrible to believe that Christ was not in some way fully real (was not fully man, for example)?

C: We shall, I hope, be getting on to that later; but I can at least say at present that the main reason why the Church so perspicaciously set itself against that heresy was because it made nonsense of Christ's being a saviour. And so I ask: in what sense was Gautama a saviour?

CB: There's nothing mysterious here. He saves us through his teachings. When he is gone from earthly existence, his Teaching, his *Dhamma*, remains with us, as he said. He helps us because he is the supreme example of humanity that we know in this age, because he achieved Enlightenment and taught us how too we may gain the ultimate insight and peace.

JB: Yes, the Buddha intervenes in human history in his teaching. He does not, precisely, *perform* anything in order to save mankind. Or at least, this is the first truth which we were taught to grasp. But we recognize also that those who are destined for Buddhahood can give us of their overflowing treasury of merit in order that we may be assisted along the Way.

M: I wouldn't agree that this properly expresses the truth about God; but I can see that it *echoes* the truth about God. For Allah is the Compassionate One, the Merciful. Whom He wishes to assist He may. It is up to Him. This doubtless is the grain of truth preserved in the idea of the Bodhisattva who can, in effect, confer grace upon ordinary men, and in the idea of the Western Paradise, to which one can, according to some Buddhist teachers, be translated—provided only that one calls on the name of the Buddha. But on the other hand, one can hardly look with favour upon this notion of the Tathāgata appearing upon earth. This looks like a blasphemous identification of God with man—or with the appearance of man, I don't care which.

C: We keep getting back to this point; but perhaps we should leave it on one side for the moment, as we shall have to discuss the notion of Incarnation at a later stage. But it would be interesting to decide what the likenesses and unlikenesses are between the Three-Body doctrine and the Trinity doctrine. I can see how there's some analogy between the transformation body and the human nature of Christ. But I'm not sure how the other two items fit.

JB: The celestial Buddhas express something which we find in the belief in God as the Heavenly Father. This of course is especially so in regard to the idea that the Buddha Amitābha can translate the faithful to his Western Paradise. And you spoke a lot earlier about belief in God as arising from, and resting upon, intimations of the numinous. I suspect that our picturesque imagery of the many celestial Buddhas is connected with these. As for the Absolute, this is the essence of Buddhahood and in a sense resides in each one of us, for we are all going in that direction eventually. Would it be absurd to see here an echo of the Christian belief in the Holy Spirit?

C: But there is something a little impersonal about this merging with the Absolute—though I suspect that some of your Mahāyānists hint at a personality lying, so to speak, in the heart of the Absolute. Another point: you speak of *many* celestial Buddhas, and isn't this a disguised polytheism?

JB: But if one can have many earthly Buddhas why shouldn't there be many celestial ones? And it isn't as though only one person has become Enlightened! Remember, too, that all Buddhas are ultimately one, in the Absolute, in their *dharmakāya*. So what may look to you at first polytheistic is at heart monistic.

J: I think you're wise to use the term 'monistic' rather than 'monotheistic' here. For as far as I can see, though your Three-Body doctrine bears some analogy to Christian theism, it nevertheless is ultimately not really theistic. For the goal is still Buddhahood: or translating it into our terms, Godhood. And so it cuts across a basic sentiment in theism, as we have more than once emphasized. Your worship of celestial Buddhas, your heeding of the wonderful and compassionate sacrifices of the Bodhisattvas, your reception of merit from them, your hopes of rebirth in a Western Paradise—all these, though in practice they seem to come close to theism and to the religion of devotion and worship, at least in theory remain subsidiary and auxiliary. They are aids towards the future state of each one of us, namely Buddhahood. Thus your system of thought is basically very like that of Śaṅkara's: and it was not for nothing that he was accused of being a crypto-Buddhist. That's my reading of the situation. Am I correct?

JB: Yes, I suppose so. Certainly our metaphysicians tend to take the *via negativa* in describing the Absolute, as names like *Tathatā* and *Śūnyatā* already show. They point to its transcendent ineffability. Nevertheless, at a lower level the Absolute does manifest itself in a personal way, in the historical and celestial Buddhas. There are, then, certain analogies to the Advaita, though it should be noted that we do not ascribe to the celestial Buddhas the precise creative functions which the Advaita ascribes to the *Iśvara*.

M: It's astonishing that Buddhism should have developed thus in two so different directions.

JB: But are they fundamentally different? The Mahāyāna retains all the essentials of the Theravāda, but fills them out. Rebirth, impermanence, *anattā, nirvāṇa*—all these ideas remain. Where we really differ most from the Lesser Vehicle is in the new richness the notion of Buddhist *karuṇā* acquires. There is here not only a moving away from what often seems to us the self-centred career of the *arhat*, towards the ideal of universal Buddhahood, which presents before our eyes the need of all men for help in salvation; but also the Bodhisattva becomes the ideal of strenuous and compassionate sacrifice on behalf of others. The career of the Buddha-to-be is often painted in terms which are most reminiscent of Christ's life and teaching. And this loving compassion is for all men to attain, if they can but realize the basic one-ness of existence. There is a single spiritual Reality pervading everything, which unites us all: no man is an island. This is the living importance of our teaching about the *dharmakāya*. Within us all lies the spark which can, if nurtured, blossom forth into the luminosity of Enlightenment.

C: Christ in us, Buddha in us—I can see the unity of insight. Yet what a difference of emphasis also! The *bodhi* which all can eventually attain isn't that loving communion with God which we preach. For finally, according to your teaching, one goes beyond the Tathāgata, beyond the personal God, and merges unrecognizably in the Absolute. But we've already seen (in discussing Śaṅkara) where our disagreements lie in regard to this. Yet I recognize that in practice the Mahāyāna can bear an astounding similarity to the teachings of Christianity. This convinces me that everywhere men can gain remarkable insights into the Truth. But there is Christ: He is the stumbling-block, for the historicity of His stupendous claims and deeds is beyond question.

JB: Now, possibly, you're being unfair. You can't simply speak of 'historicity' like that. Certainly we don't deny that Christ lived on earth (and in this sense you don't deny the historicity of the Buddha). But Christ's claims are not self-authenticating. There are, as we have seen, certain presuppositions which have to be accepted before the claims can be substantiated as they stand. And these presuppositions will be repudiated by Jews and Muslims, to mention no others.

M: Yes, we've been skating round this subject for some time now, and I feel that it ought to be tackled before we go any further. For here we encounter a deep disagreement which modifies our respective views very considerably. But first could I delineate a monotheist's feeling about the Three-Body doctrine and its associated conceptions? In a way, I feel that C has been too complaisant. And this is simply because of the undoubted likenesses between Mahāyānist and Christian beliefs. But remember that we Muslims must remain exceedingly unhappy (to put the matter no more strongly) at the idea of the Buddha as a manifestation of the Absolute, if indeed the Absolute represents something rather analogous to God. Nor can we approve the proliferation of legendary Buddhas, for in practice this means polytheism. Their theoretical unity in the *dharmakāya* hardly seems sufficient guarantee of the purity of monotheism.

JB: We're back to our earlier disagreements about the

importance of this kind of religious purity! Our system has its pluralistic aspects, and this in a way should comfort you, since you criticized Śaṅkara's absolute monism. But it fits together in a single traditional framework that has stood the test of time. And ultimately it has the greatest simplicity. If you wish to reduce it to its bare essentials, it can be looked on as saying that the Absolute manifests itself in the phenomenal realm in the guise of the Tathāgata. And this is surely a simple enough doctrine. But of course you have an objection to this very idea of *manifestation*. Yet doesn't God reveal Himself in visions and the like? Are these not manifestations? Or again, does not God manifest Himself in historical events, according to you? Why then should the Divine Being not manifest Himself upon earth in the form of an Enlightened One?

M: It's too much like the doctrine of the Incarnation for my liking! Or rather, not for my liking, but for Allah's liking: for I only follow the teachings of the Holy Qu'rān. So can we get on to discussing the Incarnation?

VI

INCARNATION AND HISTORY

H: I suspect that C is going to be under fire from two directions. On the one hand, there are those like the Muslims who repudiate the very notion that a human can be divine, can literally be God. For this is blasphemous from his point of view. On the other hand, there are those who feel, as did Gandhi, that the very *uniqueness* of the Incarnation constitutes a stumbling-block.

JB: I for one would not be averse to allowing that perhaps Christ is a Bodhisattva. But He cannot be thought to be unique in this respect.

C: I find these remarks strange. You feel there is something wrong in the singleness of Christ. But if God has become man, and if there be one God, then . . .

JB: How strong is this argument? Surely we recognize that God can appear at sundry times and places, that He can manifest Himself in various guises. Why should one object to this idea? We believe in one Absolute, one *dharmakāya*, but this doesn't prevent us from conceiving of a multiplicity of Buddhas.

M: This is all very interesting, to be sure; but it is not fundamental. The fundamental question which we ought to ask ourselves is whether we ought to allow *any* human being to be called Divine. Surely it is a repudiation of the central notion of monotheism, however it may be covered up by such doctrinal subtleties as the Trinity doctrine and the Three-Body doctrine.

C: I concede your point, that at first sight the Incarnation must seem a shocking and indeed blasphemous belief, and I can't altogether blame those Jews at the time of Jesus who thought of His claims as an infringement of the fundamental basis of their religion. Certainly one couldn't expect anyone to predict with accuracy the form which God's intervention was going to take. One or two of the Prophets had a deeper understanding. But I agree that the Incarnation was amazing, incredible, hard to accept, a stumbling-block, a scandal.

J: But it's not enough to say this is it? The fact that something is *incredible* can hardly count as an argument for its truth! There must be other reasons upon which you rely. I don't, of course, want to imply that these matters are decided by cerebration; yet surely there must be relevant considerations and insights! And although you think that God's intervention wasn't predictable, we might still be able to make some sense of it and penetrate nearer the heart of the mystery, *ex post facto*. That, I imagine, is the line that you must take.

C: Yes: but there's so much to be said. There is the individual's experience of the living Christ, for one thing.

JB: And *we* point to the individual's experience of the Buddha! If we're to discuss these matters at all it is surely necessary, as you pointed out, to make some distinction between experience and interpretation. And this interpretation which you mention has to be argued for.

C: I stand corrected (and out of my own mouth too). Yes, I must obviously say much more. Here I think we have to go to the heart of the matter—man's need for redemption. Christ is not only like the historical Buddha, a great Teacher. He is above all Saviour and Redeemer. Now the fallen state of man is such, so deeply plunged in sin is he, so terribly cut off from God, that it's necessary . . .

H: Forgive my interrupting, but you are here presupposing a lot about sin which is not universally acceptable.

M: And forgive me for interrupting too, but you began to say 'it's necessary . . .': necessary that *what*? I hope you're not about to say that it is necessary for God to do something! Surely God is above the mere necessities of human thought.

84

C: As to H's point, this is one which we have agreed to differ about. Our different ways of looking at the world and at man are, I think we agreed, largely determined by our differing conceptions of God. As it appears, man, when confronted by the terrible purity of the All-Holy One, cannot but consider himself as other than holy, or sinful; and this feeling is considerably reinforced when we realize that moral defects are themselves a sin against God, and that man is full of immoral and evil tendencies. Man has good, divinely inspired impulses as well—but we have to be realistic in noticing our own sinfulness. But, of course, the Indian emphasis upon ignorance, in which the soul becomes clouded with desire, gives us a different picture; and we have agreed to differ on this. Now as to your point, M, I'm well aware that my way of expressing myself was bad. I was about to say that it is necessary, if man is to be redeemed, for the gap between him and God to be bridged in some way. Perhaps I should say that this is what experience and revelation would appear to teach us. We have to rely here on human insights; but anyway these themselves are God-given. Now this bridging of the gap of which I have spoken cannot, assuredly, be performed by man himself. The atonement can only be performed by God.

H: These remarks are related to a whole nest of concepts like *grace* and *holiness*; and therefore can only be cogent given that a thorough-going religion of worship and devotion has been singled out as the highest truth. I say this just to remind you of our background divergences.

C: Yes, we certainly ought to keep such divergences in mind. But to proceed. On our view (which is backed by much testimony) man has no hope on his own of gaining that atonement which will bring him close to God again. Only God can do that. And if I may say so, this is why I feel uneasy at the ideas of attaining *nirvāṇa*, gaining enlightenment, realizing the Ātman and so forth. For they imply, wrongly as I believe, that man can pull himself up to holiness by his own boot-laces.

J: Both M and I will go with you thus far: that it's not

through the work of men that men attain holiness, for we are utterly dependent in this upon God's goodness.

C: Yet we also recognize that men ought to expiate their sins, for to recognize my sinfulness is also to recognize that I ought to do something about it. Just as when we have offended someone we feel that we have to perform some appropriate gesture which will go some way towards making things right, so too we feel that we ought to expiate our sins. This can be a snare and a delusion, since it can so easily lead to the view that by performing the right sacrifices or doing the right deeds we can automatically ensure that our sins are covered. Still, it's an inescapable sentiment, to my mind: expiation and repentance go together. Thus the conclusion out of all this is that it would be marvellously appropriate if both God and man together can wash away human sin. Only God can save: only man can expiate. The wonderful love of God is displayed in the fact that God becomes man in order to save mankind on behalf of mankind!

M: But surely this is a derogation of the divine power. That was what I was hinting at earlier. God is not forced to save man thus or thus.

C: I quite agree. How else would Christ's actions display a love which is not compelled? Of course God was not forced to adopt this means of redemption. But we can see how wonderfully appropriate it is, once we can get over our dumbfounded amazement that God can become man at all!

H: But if you're allowing that God didn't need to appear in this form upon earth, you can surely allow that there's no necessity about the *uniqueness* of the Incarnation.

C: I'm not saying that there's some absolute necessity. But there are various points to bear in mind. First, the whole logic (if I may speak thus) of Christ's sacrifice is that He was fully man. Unless he had been, then he couldn't be in that state of solidarity with mankind which allows Him to take our sins upon Himself and which demonstrates the supreme love of

God for His creatures. I suspect that in your Indian beliefs (the avatars of Viṣṇu and the appearances of Buddhas) there is a tendency to consider them to be merely *manifestations* of God, and not to think of them as though God *really is* this person. Of course, any flavour of unreality about the world will attach itself to such figures; and thus Buddhist metaphysical idealism is not unconnected with the notion of the historical Buddha as a mere (and almost magical) *appearance*. But we Christians must believe in the full humanity, that is to say, reality, of Christ. There have, true enough, been strivings towards docetism in certain times during the Church's history. But the Church has wisely repudiated them as heretical.

J: And to what do you ascribe these strivings?

C: To a variety of causes, I suppose: but perhaps the most important was the sentiment which we just now noted—that the affirmation of Christ's divinity, as a separate Person, seems to cut across the main principle of monotheism. And docetism is a way of escaping from this, for if Christ was a mere appearance, then we don't need the doctrine of the Trinity; and we don't come up against this great paradox that God is both God and man.

J: I'm happy to hear you saying all this, for it squares with my own beliefs. But you were offering to give a number of reasons for not having many incarnations: perhaps you want to go on with them.

C: Yes; but there's something more to be said about the first one. That is, my suggestion that there is an air of unreality about Indian variants of belief in incarnation is borne out to some degree by the very use of such terms as *avatāra* and *nirmāṇakāya*, since *descent* (into human or animal form) and *transformation* do suggest that God or the Absolute isn't thoroughly identified with such earthly forms. Perhaps too the idea of multiple incarnation ties in with belief in rebirth, for this already conditions us to the idea of different individuals as being linked together in a mysterious way, of different bodies harbouring the same spirit, and so on.

H: But one can certainly believe in rebirth without being a Vaiṣṇavite or a Mahāyānist.

C: Yes; but my chief point remains: that the uniqueness of Christ's Incarnation is a sign of His full humanity. But further, though I sympathize a lot with the Indian attitude to animals, it does seem wrong for us to believe that God could ever appear in animal form. This *does* seem blasphemous.

M: Indeed it does! But this may just be a further indication of the danger of compromising over monotheism.

C: Your remark puts another thought into my head— perhaps, you may think, a rather *formal* point: but our Christian belief does represent the simplest form of a doctrine of Incarnation. Once we cross the border from what you Muslims would call pure monotheism, we might at first think that there's no reason why there shouldn't be many incarnations, but at least we Christians preserve the purest, the simplest, belief about the matter. If we're going to allow that other things being equal one should prefer the simpler doctrine, then this principle certainly favours Christian doctrine over against the Vaiṣṇavite beliefs. But it is, as I say, rather a formal consideration. And perhaps you gentlemen have detected a certain unrealism about my way of arguing about Christ. For above all my belief rests upon *historical* evidence. There's a limit to the amount of useful discussion we can have which ignores this primary fact. For I agree that Christian doctrine is an *apparent* derogation of monotheism: and therefore no one ought to affirm this seemingly blasphemous paradox, that God became man, without trepidation. And what assuages the trepidation is the historical evidence.

H: Now one of the main Hindu objections to orthodox Christianity must necessarily come to the surface. For the very fact that historical evidence is so important tells us something significant—that your beliefs are bound up with a special view of history. They are bound up with the idea that God works out his purpose in history; with the notion that God has a Chosen People, who if they sometimes stray from the right path, nevertheless prepare the way for a particular historical Saviour; with the conception of God channelling His activity through a people and through a Person. Some of all this we have already discussed, in connection with the notion of purpose and direction in history; but at the present moment I'm chiefly concerned with the scandalous particularity involved in Christian belief.

C: Is that so absurd?

H: The idea strikes me as unattractive. For think what it implies. It implies that we have to look to a particular time and place for our salvation. Despite the fact that there have been in other times and other places a number of luminous spiritual teachers, we have to direct all our attention and devotion to Christ. And this means that many, many people who have in the present and past not heard the Gospel lose the most precious thing in the world.

C: But your own ancient traditions about the appearance of world teachers tell us that such lights of the world are to be expected to arise in *Jambudvīpa*, in the Indian sub-continent. Isn't this also the Chosen People idea?

H: But remember that India was vaguely thought of as the whole world (as in the West the Roman Empire constituted 'the whole civilized world' for a long time). But in any event our feeling for multiplicity does allow us to think that there may be great Teachers elsewhere. And our emphasis on inner enlightenment and individual insight does rather suggest that knowledge of God doesn't have to be channelled through a particular historical figure. It does seem absurd that salvation should come through a particular person. For don't we all have some sort of access? Or, looking at it from the other end, why should God favour one people with His revelation and not others?

C: I recognize that our view must seem 'foolishness to the Hindus'; but if God does reveal Himself in history, then He must reveal Himself in *particular* history. History is of its nature particular. And so, whether Christ had appeared in Palestine or in Japan, there would still have been the scandal of particularity. It mustn't be thought that we of the Western tradition who have benefited more directly and intimately from God's self-revelation are claiming any sort of credit or superiority. But God, having chosen those who had benefited from and perceived His graciousness, worked out His ultimate purpose in the same context. It's true that some people at certain times have seemingly been deprived of this consummation of God's revelation, but the ways of God are inscrutable; and their salvation rests, not with our opinions, but with Him.

CB: Your last remarks are so much as to say that the scandal of particularity does constitute some sort of argument against Christianity, but that, God being mysterious, it doesn't constitute a knock-down argument.

C: Yes, I suppose that I'm saying that. I don't deny that the scandal in question *is* a scandal. But I can't help but feel that wherever a religion goes back to a historical teacher (and Buddhism does) or to a certain historical tradition (and surely Hinduism looks back to the Veda), you're bound to get particularism. Now all the great religions are in some way or other traditional; so that we're all equally implicated in this scandal.

H: We're all implicated, perhaps—but not *equally*! Hinduism and Buddhism, at least in their higher manifestations, aren't merely traditional but are also in a real sense *experimental*. Although we must start with traditions, it is also necessary to transcend them, and each man must ultimately work out his own salvation with diligence.

J: And we have already seen, in our earlier discussions, that there are objections to this way of looking at things. For if we believe in God, we don't suppose that salvation is simply a matter of our going and working it out. Of course, we have to make an effort (if we are good, a supreme effort) to act and think and live in accordance with the Will of God. But we really mustn't suppose that we can thereby ensure salvation. Our spiritual health ultimately depends upon God. For it is only the Holy One that can make us holy. Hence we reject this 'experimental' religion which is so often to be discovered in the Orient.

H: But certainly experience is relevant to our discovery of the Truth, is it not?

J: There is the experience of God's goodness and power; but this experience teaches us that the initiative is with God. It does not lie with us. It is not for us to go 'experimenting'.

H: But surely we can talk of a search for God? It's true that having found God you may wish to say, or feel compelled to say, that it was God in you which impelled you upon the search —that the very quest was itself a sign that you had found God already or rather that God had found you. I can understand all this, for do not some of our *bhakti* theologians say that salvation is like the way a cat carries its kittens, by lifting them up and transporting them by the scruff of the neck? Yes, I understand your point of view. But surely we can make a preliminary distinction between ordinary (and non-religious) conduct on the one hand and that behaviour which displays a real desire to find the ultimate Truth on the other? And don't we have to recognize that religion links up with life, that its truth has to be tested in living and in experience? In this sense at least, religion must be experimental.

C: Here again we're back at a certain difference of emphasis between our respective points of view. For although assuredly the divine must have some impact in experience (we all believe that), the picture of experimental religion is one where man takes the initiative. And this is something which (though it can be conceded in a qualified sense) runs counter to our ideas about God, about the Living God. Perhaps it is because spiritual techniques of meditation and so forth have been so subtly and elaborately developed in India that you so often think of insight as being something which man of his own unaided efforts can attain.

H: Not always do we think thus, and it is most interesting that orthodox Yoga itself recognizes the importance of the concept of *Īśvara* or Lord. Perhaps it's because the quest for ultimate happiness, bliss or serenity is in a peculiar way self-stultifying, since exclusive concentration upon achieving this goal is liable to introduce the wrong motives and so to cut across the requirement that one should be detached.

JB: Though I said I would exclude Zen from my remarks I cannot refrain from observing there that this comment of yours is most reminiscent of Zen teachings. Have you read E. Herrigel's beautiful book *Zen in the Art of Archery*? You may recall that Zen is (oddly enough and among other things) taught through the practice of archery: and one of the lessons emphasized (indeed perhaps it's the supreme lesson) is that one should be able to hit the target without aiming! This seems absurd; and yet some masters of archery apparently attain to this accomplishment. And the point of it is that just as one hits the bull without aiming, so one attains peace without aiming at *it*. And this, whatever else you may think about the doctrines (or non-doctrines!) of Zen, is a profound psychological insight.

H: However, this is but an aside. But I concede to C that the subtle techniques of meditation of all sorts which we have evolved do suggest that men can, by training themselves in the right way, gain purity of consciousness, insight and so on. But isn't this something of credit to the Indian religious tradition? One great worry, in my experience, among Europeans is that religion represents certain doctrines; but there is so little practical guidance on how to go about salvation.

C: I would dispute that. It's true that we don't suggest to our faithful such practices as Yoga or mindfulness (in the Buddhist sense). But there is *The Practice of the Presence of God* by Brother Lawrence, together with many, many other such practical and spiritual guides. And the heart of Christianity, moreover, lies in the imitation of Christ. This imitation consists in following One who not only preached the love of one's neighbour but also displayed in His career the tragically realistic truth about moral behaviour; that one must requite evil with good, that one must turn the other cheek, that true goodness takes the form of sacrifice.

J: Sacrifice? Earlier I heard you say something about atonement. Are you meaning 'sacrifice' in the religious sense?

One strand at least of Christian doctrine seems to be that Christ through His sacrifice upon the cross brought mankind into a state of atonement with God. And your remarks about expiation suggested that Christ is believed to have performed a ritual or quasi-ritual expiation on behalf of mankind. On the other hand, what you just now said about sacrifice is specifically moral, as I understand it, in character. I mean: we sometimes talk about sacrifice in a purely *secular* context, where sacrifice is a moral concept referring to the valuation of one's own interests as drastically lower than those of others—where one gives up something important in order to serve others. I'm not clear as whether there's a close connection between this moral sense of 'sacrifice' and the religious meaning.

C: 'The sacrifices of God are a broken spirit', so it is said. But maybe there's a distinction such as the one you outline. You may recall that at an earlier point I advocated a distinction between the numinous and the mystical; and so now I wouldn't be adverse, if you so wish it, to differentiating between those insights which are purely moral and those which are religious in character. This may appear strange to those who are accustomed to thinking of morality as necessarily bound up with religion; I myself believe that one can best make sense of morality by appealing to religion. Nevertheless there's clearly some sort of distinction between merely moral questions and those which are religious. (Although religion, in its way, absorbs morality, it's still theoretically possible to have morality without religion, as is testified by the lives of certain extraordinarily good agnostics.) Now certainly, seen from a secular viewpoint, sacrifice is as you described it, a valuation of one's own interests as of less importance, in some particular context, than those of one's neighbour's. And implicit in moral action is the principle that one should, where the opportunity offers, be patient in adversity and requite good for evil. Perhaps one can consistently adhere to the principle of 'Turn the other cheek' without belief in God. But surely Christ's sacrifice *illuminates* this principle. Even if, from the secular point of view, Christ's action of being a Saviour is not *simply* moral, in that one has to appeal to concepts here such as *atonement* which are not simply ethical in character, but contain religious implications, nevertheless the two sides of Christ's sacrifice hang together, do they not? They reaffirm that harmony between true religion and the higher morality in a wonderful way. They show how the two great commandments to love God and to love one's neighbour are closely intertwined.

J: So I take it that you're saying not merely that Christ saves us but that he illuminates the heart of morality? But the Jewish tradition already knew these two great commandments. Was it necessary for God to reaffirm them in action?

C: Again, no: it was not *necessary*, for nothing is necessary for God in this way. Rather, I'm trying to show how the Christian message hangs together. Being men, we can't penetrate to the full meaning of the Mystery—but we can gain a deep insight into the pattern of existence by seeing the way these teachings hang together.

JB: I, for one, do not deny the splendid example of Christ's love. But this example is, as you know, illustrated elsewhere and equally clearly—many of our stories of the Buddhas-to-be illustrate the deepest heroic compassion. Buddhist *karuṇā* and Christian love go hand in hand. As we said earlier, this is one of the great resemblances between Christianity and the Great Vehicle.

C: Yet this is where we get back to the problem of historicity. For luminous as many of your legends may be, there is no real assurance that the displays of 'heroic compassion' actually occurred.

JB: This is where I present you with a dilemma, and I hope it's not an unfair one. For either there are and have been Bodhisattvas who have performed these wonderful deeds, in which case your argument falls to the ground; or the stories are imaginative ways of saying something about God's nature, in which case they show that Eastern men, independently of the Christian revelation, have seen the truth. And if so, why is it necessary for God also to reveal Himself in history? Perhaps, as I suggested before, He was a Bodhisattva!

C: But I still rest my case on history. I'm impressed by the Great Vehicle, for it shows how men in different parts of the world have groped their way towards the Truth; but the fact that God has revealed Himself elsewhere than in Palestine and Christendom doesn't imply that He did not literally intervene in history in the way we claim. And so far from wishing to criticize the teachings of the Mahāyāna, I'm comforted by its shining example. For to my mind it shows that mankind was unable to remain within the confines of the simple but austere teachings of the Theravāda, but thirsted for a deeper and a richer faith. Obscurely, Eastern men here thirsted for Christ.

J: I'm not sure how strong this argument from thirsting is: men have thirsted after idolatry as well as after righteousness.

JB: Perhaps; but we must begin with the experience of men. Not that I'm too happy about C's argument, since it can be reversed—by saying that Christianity shows how Western men have groped after the deep and rich faith of the Great Vehicle!

C: But I cannot look at it that way, because of my claim about the uniqueness of Christ. And here, to repeat myself (I hope not *ad nauseam*), I rest my case on history.

CB: In view of the fact that you *are* repeating yourself, perhaps this is a suitable point at which to shift the focus of the discussion. This universe is vast and incredibly complicated. Amid the millions of stars in each of the millions of galaxies it's not improbable that there is life. Both the rich Buddhist picture of the cosmos and modern science hint at the possibility of life on other worlds. Not in this solar system, but in some solar system elsewhere. It may well be; and we shouldn't blind ourselves to such possibilities. Now, it may be that there are beings capable of salvation in some corner of the universe for ever inaccessible to mankind. But the Gospel could not, *ex hypothesi*, be carried thither. I agree that neither could the Buddha's teaching; but we recognize a plurality of Buddhas and there's no reason why someone on that distant planet should not gain Enlightenment. Now, if the Gospel can't be carried there, then those beings are cut off from the Saviour. This suggests that God might perhaps become incarnate also on that distant planet. But then what of this supposed simplicity which attaches to Christian doctrine?

C: This is all quite speculative. We don't *know* of the existence of such beings.

CB: But surely we must envisage this possibility. And if we do, then we envisage the possibility that God becomes man elsewhere in the universe.

H: And then what happens to the Trinity doctrine? The Trinity formula is supposed to be the final truth about God's nature. But we would have to think in terms of a Quaternity or more, wouldn't we?

C: As far as we can see, the Trinity doctrine is the final truth about God, though I allow that we cannot fully penetrate into this truth.

H: But you recognize that this truth is in some sense provisional, since we don't know that there are not reasoning beings in other parts of the cosmos?

C: To that extent, yes, it is provisional.

H: And in this way you are certainly coming closer to a traditional Hindu attitude to doctrines, and moving away from the rather rigid claims to finality which usually typify Christian dogmatics.

C: All that we can do is to receive the truth which has been revealed to us and to try to gain some insight into it. Now I don't deny that this possibility of life on other worlds leaves me in some perplexity. But I'm sure that Christianity represents the highest truth available to us. The mention of life on other worlds is just a way of re-emphasizing the scandal of particularity. I concede, as I said before, that it *is* a scandal. But despite that I still hold to Christ.

CB: You are, of course, in a somewhat favoured position. Let me explain why. If someone were to ask me how best he could work out his salvation and he were a Christian, I might well advise him to take his Christianity more seriously. In other words, we Buddhists don't object to people who remain Christians, provided that they're good Christians; but you Christians attempt rigidly to proselytize us Buddhists.

H: Yes, just as there are different schools within Hinduism, so I can conceive that other religions ought to be treated in the same manner—as different ways to the Truth.

C: Once again we get back to different conceptions of religious truth. But I certainly do wish to go some of the way towards your position. One thing revealed by our present discussions is that there is some agreement on certain aspects of religious truth; and another thing which has become obvious is that even revealed and dogmatic religion has to be defended. It's not enough to say 'Take it on faith or leave it'. This is obvious, I say, and especially when one great faith meets with another. But even if I recognize that our Christian belief is not self-evidently true, I still hold that *par excellence* it is the truth, not merely because of general principles, but also because of the historical facts.

JB: Since this appeal to history keeps coming between us and agreement, could you say some more, not about the general presuppositions of Christ's divinity (for we have touched upon these) but about the way in which the actual historical evidence is relevant? For how can particular pieces of historical evidence actually establish the divinity of a human being? I know that you're going to ask me a similar question about Buddhahood! But we may have different ideas as to what evidence counts.

C: Well, first, Christ's life, though it didn't conform to the pattern expected by most people at the time, does show Him to be the Messiah.

JB: Likewise, Gautama's life and characteristics display him as a luminous successor to the previous Enlightened Ones.

J: And *we* deny that Jesus was Messiah!

C: Which goes to show that I must say much more. Now Christ worked miracles. Not all of those which are reported in the Gospel writings may be substantiated, but some of them certainly are true, such as some of the miracles of healing. But above all there is the fact of the Resurrection, which demonstrates Christ's victory over death.

M: If indeed he was ever crucified! As you know, Muslim tradition denies his death on the cross, though the Qu'rān speaks of his ascension.

C: Let's not get down to detailed historical investigation. What we want to see is how historical events (or, if you like, alleged historical events) give us clues about the transcendent. Christ's miracles are intimations of the underlying omnipotence which was His, and the Resurrection tells us of His status as Saviour of mankind. Then again, His teachings hint at the divine omniscience. Above all, His supreme goodness reminds of God's holiness.

CB: Except for the Resurrection, you could use similar arguments about Gautama Buddha, for he displayed the gifts which you mention. Of course, I'm not much concerned about the legendary and miraculous episodes which surround the Buddha's life, since it's above all his Enlightenment and lucid teachings to which we Buddhists look.

C: But miracles require good evidence. Then again, the course of Christ's life doesn't only display the supreme love of God but it also fits into a historical situation, into a pattern of history; and thus we Christians see His life as the key to God's purpose as it is worked out in history. But I realize full well, from what we've said earlier, that not all of you will accept this attitude to human history. Perhaps it would be worthless for us now to repeat our former arguments.

H: Agreed; but it's good that you have mentioned our divergences at this juncture, for they point to different emphases in different theologies; and we can see how the structure of our respective beliefs is very closely tied to the diverse pictures of the nature of the transcendent Being. Perhaps too this is an appropriate place to note the considerations which we have seen to be relevant in a discussion of the Incarnation. On the one hand, the rigid monotheists object to the doctrine root and branch, on the ground that it is blasphemous to identify God with any human being: it is setting up another god beside God. On the other hand, we Indians rather feel that the Christian insistence on the uniqueness of the Incarnation is too exclusive, since it means that God channels His activity through a particular people and a particular tradition. In this connection we noted that there may be life on other worlds, and this presents greater perplexities for Christianity than, I think, for any other religion, and seems rather to weaken the principle of simplicity which is one of the arguments for uniqueness. Still, empirically (looking at the world faiths as we find them), Christianity does have the simplest doctrine of Incarnation. Moreover, we have seen that Christians, in line with the emphasis upon purity of worship, etc., do object to animal *avatāras* and the like, as being blasphemous (here the argument reverts to the issue which we raised first of all, namely the question of what attitude is the best one to adopt in regard to polytheism). In addition, however, Christians consider the full humanity of Christ to be of the greatest moment, for it displays God's ineffable love that He should empty Himself: and further, without full humanity Christ cannot genuinely be in a state of solidarity with mankind, and only thus can He bear men's sins. These considerations involve reference to ideas of sin, sacrifice, expiation and so on, which may not be accorded the same weight in religions which do not so emphatically lay stress upon the numinous aspect of spiritual truth.

C: Yes, I recall that it was said that the doctrine of Original Sin is partly a reflection of our idea of God, since the holiness of the All-Holy gives us a lively sense of our own imperfection. Also it is linked to the moral sense, since sin can be viewed as a case of moral defect (rather than religious impurity). It was also said that our view of history ties in with the sense of contingency, which again refers us to the power and creativity of the One God. These things show us, as you say, how we trace back many of our divergences to different conceptions of God. Our notions are woven subtly together.

CB: Don't forget non-conceptions about God. Don't leave *me* out! Also, we mustn't omit reference to different conceptions about man: remember that we remarked upon the harmony between the cyclical view of history and the doctrine of rebirth (both are implicit in the notion of *saṁsāra*).

H: Since so much of the Christian argument (for example) turns on the supposed need for salvation through the agency of God, we must include among the divergent conceptions which influence our theological thinking the thesis that men can of their own endeavour attain salvation—a view which is to be found in the Theravāda, in some versions of the Mahāyāna and in some forms of Hindu doctrine, to mention no others.

J: Let us not get confused here. The doctrine of rebirth definitely concerns living beings within the cosmos; but certainly on the other hand the respective views of mankind represented by the theories that man needs grace or other supernatural aid and that man can gain salvation through his own efforts are partly, if not wholly, determined by beliefs about God. This is clear from the fact that the crux of the matter is whether men receive divine aid in their strivings. And the notion of divine help is only appropriate where we have a *personal* concept of God's nature, a concept which also fits in with the numinous experience as revealing a terrible and *dynamic* entity which confronts mankind. Thus we can make a distinction: whereas the view of man represented by the doctrines of reincarnation and rebirth is definitely about life within the cosmos and doesn't so far need any reference to Something transcending the universe, the main motive for saying that man needs outside help is that the Divine Being presents Himself to mankind as a Holy Being, with whom the initiative in salvation must lie. In brief: rebirth concerns this world; the need for help refers to the transcendent realm.

Consequently, while rebirth doctrine does not in any obvious way stem from a view about the transcendent Reality, our differences about the need for outside help are necessarily connected with divergent conceptions regarding the Holy. I think this point needs to be made for the sake of clarity.

C: Yes, indeed. As I hinted earlier, it seems to me that the Hindu and Buddhist ideas of salvation are sometimes or at least partly in consonance with Christian beliefs about the next life, even though the Christian cannot accept the doctrine of rebirth. The Hindu and Buddhist views of life in this world differ from ours; but these views are partly independent of any higher doctrines about the nature of transcendent Reality.

M: Yet J is really engaging in a digression. Suffice it it say that mainly our differences are due to different conceptions of ultimate Reality: these in turn arise from divergent emphases. We have at any rate seen some of the motives for doctrines of incarnation. It is likewise clear as to why Muslims and Jews reject the beliefs of Christians, Hindus and Buddhists alike.

C: The purity of monotheism, is it? But Christianity remains monotheistic, thanks to Athanasius!

JB: Why not then say that Buddhism remains monotheistic through the Three-Body formula?

C: Monotheistic? Monistic, rather, since *theism* involves a whole-heartedly personalistic view of the Deity. But I (regretfully perhaps) see the barb in your remark.

JB: There was no barb intended.

C: Sometimes the innocent sallies are the most telling. I see that Christianity doesn't at first sight seem purely monotheistic, since we believe in three Persons. But then one might object that the Advaita isn't *really* monistic, since it involves the two concepts of Brahman and Ātman, not to mention the two aspects of Brahman. Maybe all this indicates that in our richer systems of doctrine there are intellectual difficulties—how Three can be One, how the Ātman can be Brahman, how the

Tathāgata can be the Absolute, and so on. But paradoxes are not fatal to religion. Religion has to deal in apparent contradiction, for words are not adequate to describe the ultimate Mystery.

CB: Yet difficulties of this sort *are* difficulties. It is a *prima facie* disadvantage if a creed involves some great paradox.

C: We have been here before. The luminous austerity of the Theravāda may not be rich enough to cover the complications of Reality.

CB: But other things being equal, one prefers the simpler hypothesis, as we've agreed. Neither the Mahāyāna nor Christianity seems the simpler hypothesis.

M: Why speak of the Theravāda? Islam is magnificently simple.

C: Christianity is the simplest complicated doctrine! But we're still talking too abstractly. The events of Christ's life are where I take my stand.

H: *Impasse.* And it's good to know where it is.

C: Christianity, because of Christ's life, shows us how to overcome evil in a remarkable profound way.

M: That is strange! We have spent quite a time discussing God and goodness, but very little about evil.

H: We did speak about Original Sin and ignorance.

C: But M is right. We all in different ways believe that there is a solution to the evils of the world, and we should surely therefore say something to each other about these evils: and in this we'll doubtless be able to see more clearly the true nature of morality.

VII

EVIL AND GOOD

CB: In talking about evil I suppose we ought to begin with its origin. Now you Christians believe in an Evil Spirit, a fallen angel who somehow set the creation awry. Of necessity we Buddhists are precluded from such a doctrine, since we do not enquire about the origin of creation, as being a topic which is not conducive to salvation. It does seem odd to take such a story very seriously. It's true that the Enlightened One was tempted, under the Bo Tree, by Māra, the Tempter; and so doubtless Satan also stands for some psychological reality. But it does seem presumptuous to claim to know not merely the details of the Creation itself but also the goings-on behind the scenes, when Satan rebelled and so forth.

C: You don't like it if we prefer the story form? It's already been pointed out that the myth of the Creation is analogical history; and so I suppose is the story of the Fall of the angels and of the Fall of Adam. But these accounts give a convincing explanation of the origin of evil. For how can a perfectly good God cause all the suffering which we see around us? Aren't we right in thinking that things have gone awry?

H: Why shouldn't God be both Creator and Destroyer? For all its apparent barbarity the image of Kālī has its inherent attraction. God is beyond good and evil. This is an aspect of His omnipotence. How can you gainsay this?

C: It depends what you mean by 'beyond good and evil'. For I believe that God is beyond good, in the sense that the word 'good' which we use here gives a false impression, since it is used primarily of creatures. And the goodness of creatures is but a poor reflection of the transcendent goodness which must be found in God. But it seems all wrong for me to say that God is in some excessive way evil also. God is above all a good God.

H: Even the Devil can quote scripture, so don't object if I refer to the story of Abraham and Isaac and to the tribulations of Job. Have you not referred to God as terrible? Terribly good, perhaps, but still terrible, inspiring fear.

J: God may demand absolute obedience, but we still believe Him to be supremely good: what is wrong is our human conception of goodness, and thereby we sometimes think that we see God's actions as wrong. But God is the source of all that is good, and it's absurd and sinful of us to presume to question this goodness.

C: Yes. But I can see an inner plausibility in the Hindu view. For the yogin and the ascetic is often spoken of, in Hindu writings, as 'beyond good and evil'—that is, he is beyond ordinary duties. So it is perhaps natural (in our inveterate anthropomorphic way: who can escape it?) to ascribe to God also this sublime transcendence of matters of duty. God is above duty, above *dharma*. And this can surely be a noble doctrine. I am reminded of St Augustine's 'Love God and do what you like'.

M: And yet I do not detect a flavour of withdrawal from the world in this? Or at least in the Hindu idea?

H: I certainly agree that this notion of going beyond good and evil is not unconnected with the career of the *sannyāsin* who leaves aside ordinary duties in his pursuit of spiritual insight. Since, in Hinduism at least, moral duty has been so tightly woven into the fabric of social obligation, it's not surprising that the going beyond good and evil has at the same time been a going beyond society—into the jungle or forest, to find solitude, meditation and peace.

C: In short, we can accept this ideal of 'beyond good and evil' more easily in the context of withdrawal from the world. In this way it's easier to understand the connection between the notion of God as beyond good and evil and the concept of separation between matter and spirit that is so obvious and prominent in Hinduism and Buddhism.

CB: How so? Hinduism, yes. Buddhism, no. For we don't hold to such a distinction for the simple reason that there is no eternal Self.

C: Perhaps I was wrong to include Buddhism; and yet a distinction is made between the impermanent and the permanent, between ordinary experience and *nirvāṇa*.

CB: Let me merely say again that this is a distinction of conditions rather than of substances (so far as we learn from the Buddha's teachings). It may be that the Buddha's refusal to differentiate sharply between two sorts of substance, between matter and soul, is linked to his insistence on moral action, on conscientiousness, compassion and right behaviour. For it may have seemed that the doctrine of the eternal Self or soul encourages a certain immoral mixture of motives. At any rate, it may encourage withdrawal.

H: To each his interpretation. But if the ultimate Truth lies beyond concepts, then God lies beyond our ideas of good and evil.

C: But there's certainly a difference between our doctrine that God lies beyond 'good' and any belief that God comprehends evil in His nature.

H: It depends what's meant by 'evil'. For although we recognize the divine Being as Destroyer as well as Creator, this is partly, at least, a way of saying that what humans regard as evil is not genuinely evil. Do not some of your Christian theologians say the same thing? For if what appears to be evil to men is really good, then what objection is there to saying that God is both evil and good, provided that 'evil' and 'good' are used in their ordinary human sense? It seems to me merely a question of terminology.

C: But we have a belief in the Devil too, or at least some of us do; and this way we avoid dualism on the one hand and . . .

M: Dualism? You mean the kind of dualism found in Zoroastrianism, suggesting that there are two ultimate principles, the one good and the other evil?

C: Yes, that is what I mean. And we reject it—do we not?—because such a view denies the full power and supremacy of God. And on the other hand, belief in the Devil means that we face up to the reality of evil. You, H, appear to me in danger of falling into the thought that what appears evil isn't really so, and this you defend by pointing to the analogical sense of 'good' which is applied to God. But first, this stultifies—or may stultify—moral action. And, second, it leads to an unclear idea about the moral perfection of God.

H: Most of our ideas about God are unclear, aren't they? There is a region which lies beyond speech and beyond discursive thought.

C: But our belief about the Devil ties in with Christianity's emphasis upon the struggle in *this* world. As a practical theory, it works well, for it makes us alive to the difficulties, evils and temptations implicit in living in the world, and at the same time shows how the bad things in life are not to be attributed to God.

CB: 'Shows' is too strong a word. After all, this belief in the Devil is not absolutely well established. It may make sense of evil, in a way, given the truth of theism. But it does seem to me to be rather a stop-gap theory. Why not rather accept the view that empirical existence is intrinsically painful and that men are in their normal state deluded? In short, why not listen to the Buddha?

C: Well, it is our very concern not to blink the facts of evil that makes us feel the truth of the belief in the Devil. What is unsatisfying, to my mind, about the Buddha's insistence upon the universality of suffering is that there is no real explanation of *why* the universe is so painful.

CB: Do you not accept the explanation that suffering is the

natural concomitant of desire? And that this desire or craving is due to our lack of clear insight?

C: I can see that this is some sort of explanation. But I want to know why there is ignorance and craving, why the world is in the first instance destined for suffering.

CB: The question may be superfluous. Let's not theorize.

C: But I *want* to!

CB: You are in the grip of an intellectual craving!

C: Yet one cannot abdicate from the desire for truth. It appears to me that though our belief in a Devil looks like a stop-gap, nevertheless it helps to make sense of experience. You yourself agreed that the stories of Satan and Māra look as though they correspond at least to some psychological reality. However, I must confess that many Christians nowadays hardly take the Devil seriously. One can of course be somewhat Buddhist (if you forgive my saying so) about evil, even from within theism, and simply point to the fact of evil, hoping that the apparent contradiction with the conception of a good God will somehow be reconciled. Then one can, I suppose, ignore the Devil. But even so we still retain the idea of temptation. It is through sin and falling unto temptation that we err. We're still far from the Indian explanation in terms of ignorance.

H: Which is, you must remember, the converse of knowledge, or enlightenment or insight. This harks back to our divergences about how to dovetail the mystical and the numinous.

C: But there's another important thing to consider in this connection. You remember how we were discussing, a moment back, the question of whether it was right to think of God as 'beyond good and evil'. Although, in view of the fact that certainly our descriptions of God are analogical, one can sympathize with this view, nevertheless I failed to emphasize the positive content of our belief that God is good. For religion is interwoven with morality: worship and meditation provide the framework for daily action. Now first, how can one, as a moral being, worship a God who is not good or more than good? And second, how can one square the notion that God is the *summum bonum*, as constituting or yielding the highest bliss and happiness, with the idea of a Being who is destructive? And again, though it may often be a condition of moral power that one should at times withdraw from the world, nevertheless the moral battle has normally to be fought within the world, within the *real* world. Thus, if the conception of a Being 'beyond good and evil' links with the life of the recluse who himself at least in some measure achieves this condition, then I can propose a higher ideal than that. My view of God will reflect such an ideal. It is the ideal of the man who goes through the world, which is the world of the flesh and the Devil, and who yet, with God's grace, emerges triumphant: not unscathed, but triumphant. What I'm hinting at is this—that just as morality is part of the fabric of the best earthly existence, so too it is part of the fabric of the best transcendent existence, namely God. If so, then when we say that God is good, we mean that He is more than (humanly speaking) good.

H: Perhaps you underestimate the triumph of the recluse, for he has his battles—most severe ones.

M: And perhaps you neglect the extent to which God leads men astray, if He chooses. He is the sole arbiter of our destinies. Although the statues and other representations of Kālī, for instance, with her necklace of skulls, are very repugnant to me, as a good Muslim, I can nevertheless see some point in them. In a crude and quite inadequate (not to say blasphemous) manner they nevertheless do bring out the transcendence of God. Or at least I hope that's what they show.

C: But surely this conception of Allah's leading men astray is part and parcel of your belief in predestination, a belief which itself chimes in with and is justified by a stern emphasis upon God's transcendence and omnipotence. This is perhaps rather a different insight from that which governs the representations of God as destructive.

M: Not so very different. For at least the destructiveness of the Divine Being is a way of saying that God does what He chooses to do, without regard to human preferences. This isn't far off the doctrine of predestination. The distinction is simply that destructiveness has regard to the cosmos, predestination has regard to men. But however that may be, I seem to detect some inconsistency in your position, C. For on the one hand you admit that God is beyond our conceptions of Him; while on the other you insist that we can frame the conception of God as good. And then when we want to know what 'good' means in this context, you begin talking about morality. But ordinary human ideas about morality are, I've no doubt, laughably inadequate. Why complain if sometimes God seems to act in a way in which (morally) we don't understand?

C: I am probably at fault. Yet we have to make do with such resources as we possess. It seems to me appropriate to say that God is beyond good, because he is superbly good, not because He is 'beyond good and evil'. He is superabundantly good, and yet He is not so inaccessible that we can't recognize this. In brief, I believe that our insistence on the goodness of God ties in with the highest moral ideals. Moreover, the very agnosticism which we have to hold in part regarding the attributes of God (for they are always somewhat beyond us) can be given a moral application. First, it forces us to recognize that we must be a bit sceptical (and therefore conservative) in our moral judgments. And second, much more importantly, the insight that God is beyond ordinary standards of morality and goodness compels us to strive to transcend them. Religion thus gives substance to moral idealism. It leaves us for ever uneasy about our own virtue and wisdom and about what is required of us. One winning post in the race of virtue reveals another, and so on. But it must be held that God exceeds or transcends goodness in the direction of greater goodness, *not* that he is 'beyond good and evil'.

JB: I would certainly agree that Christianity fuses together religion and moral endeavour in a wonderful way. But so, I believe, does the Great Vehicle. However, I'm not so sure that this fusing together is as closely linked to the conception of God as a supremely perfect Person as you suggest; I sympathize with H in holding that there is a sense in which the Ultimate Reality is beyond words, and therefore 'beyond good and evil'. It is void of attributes: and that is partly why we call it the Void.

C: Nevertheless, even conceding that the highest truth about God lies in a sort of silence (which I do not fully admit)—even conceding this, the lower truth about God is also important. I feel that though characterizations of the Divine Being as destructive and as in a way evil overcome the problem of evil, they pay a heavy price: they are less exalted than the typical Jewish, Muslim and Christian conceptions.

H: Less exalted? But it's the truth, not exaltation, that we are after.

C: Yet religion and morality fuse together. Can we be satisfied with an immoral God? God comprehends everything; and it is not merely wishful thinking to suppose that He comprehends goodness.

H: And evil too, by that argument.

C: But there's a difference. God is to be worshipped and adored. And though I agree that 'evil' is a moral concept (for we must use it in our thinking about morality), yet we can't feel that we ought to choose evil. Devotion to God is a choice, a commitment. How then can we be devoted to an evil God?

H: In being devoted to Kālī one is fastening only on to a lower truth, which nevertheless hints at a higher one, as we've said—namely that human attributions do not properly apply to God.

J: Do we need to keep arguing about the degree of agnosticism about God which it is right to adopt? We have already been over this ground in other connections. But it does seem to me that the Judaic exclusiveness in matters of religion does bring forth good fruit; for we have been enabled thereby (and through God's operation) to purify our idea of God until He is not merely thought of as holy in the primary sense (as a terrible numinous Being), but He is also thought of as holy in a richer sense, where power and goodness are seen as one.

CB: It may be that the differences mentioned may have something to do with the Hindu notion of morality itself. For really there is no proper distinction in Hinduism between morality, law and religion. All three are bound together in *dharma*. Now where morality and social custom almost coincide, it is very natural to think of God as beyond them. God is not governed by social custom, not being a member of society. But this is where one is too much tied down to earth in one's thinking. Or, if you like, it's where social defects reflect themselves in a religious context. For the Hindu conception of the content of *dharma* is far too conservative and inflexible. It is bound up with the caste system. It's notable that the Buddha and other unorthodox teachers have shown a way out of the caste structure. Buddhism gives men the opportunity for equality and castelessness. I think this is a point where we begin to see that it's not sufficient to discuss the notion of evil by itself, but one must look to the practical virtues of a faith. For it appears to me that Buddhism here displays two great virtues. For on the one hand, it can be universal because the Buddha broke through the bonds which in India have tied religion down to a particular social structure. On the other hand, Buddhism provides a humanitarian ethic which doesn't depend upon speculative ideas about God's nature.

C: Let's consider your first point first: it certainly seems most important to me. My criticism of Hinduism would be that it is so socially conservative and that a lot of extraneous obligations and customs are superimposed upon morality. Indeed, it has its own kind of 'scandal of particularity'.

H: But be fair. Our society has survived many invasions and disruptions through this very social structure. And there are always correctives to social injustice and humanity. The history of Hinduism is illuminated by saints and reformers who bring us back to the best insights. Need I mention Gandhi?

C: Were not such reforming movements influenced in part by Christianity?

H: To some extent (though I find such proud claims by Westerners a little distasteful). I concede, for instance, that Gandhi learned a lot from the Sermon on the Mount. But first, it is characteristic of Hinduism to be open-minded in spiritual matters, and I do not recall instances of Christian saints who studied the scriptures of other faiths (though, I suppose, in the early days Christians learned a lot from the pagan Plato and others). And second, was the notion of *ahiṁsā*, so important not only in Gandhi's thought and life, but in Buddhism and Jainism as well, a Christian concept? Of course, there *are* texts in the Bible that point in the same direction. But has non-violence been taken so seriously in Judaism, Christianity and Islam as it has been in Hinduism and Buddhism? I think not. I further claim that Gandhi has begun to influence Westerners in their way of thinking. The traffic in moral enlightenment is not a one-way affair.

M: Nevertheless, the pattern of social custom woven into the fabric of Hinduism means that Hinduism cannot be a universal religion. It must remain the faith of a particular society or societies.

JB: Yes, it's worth remarking that however much they may diverge in methods and beliefs, Islam, Buddhism and Christianity are missionary religions in a way in which Hinduism and Judaism are not.

J: Is it a virtue to be a missionary religion?

C: Only, I think, in this sense that, a religion, if it claims to be the ultimate truth, ought to be universal. Men ought not to be excluded from salvation because they happen to belong to the wrong society.

J: But who wants to say that *that* happens?

C: Nevertheless, it turns out in practice that being a Jew or a Hindu involves certain obligations which can't be acquired from outside (or at least only with great difficulty—in some cases through inter-marriage or through long having been settled in the country in question). In practice, I can't become a Hindu.

H: But all religions have social badges; so that the practical difficulties of settling into another faith differ only in degree.

C: Differences of degree can be important. I think it's desirable that a religion should be as 'open' as possible.

J: And yet, just as the I-Thou relationship with God is an inter-personal one, that is a social one, of a sort, so religion in its practical application to this world must work in a social way. It is the task of the Jews to show how the Kingdom of God can be realized here and now.

C: To return to the question of social badges. I suppose, H, that your point was that there are various peculiar customs distinguishing the adherent of one religion from others—such as the Sikh requirement that you shouldn't cut your hair, must wear a bangle, etc. I imagine that we could also include under this head certain items in the moral code, such as the Buddhist prohibition on killing animals. Such differences often cause a lot of trouble, since what is allowable to the adherent of one faith becomes outrageous to the adherent of another. However, I imagine it would be difficult for us to reach agreement on such particularities or even decide how one would set about reaching such agreement. On the other hand, we would probably all concur in general that where there are such differences in religious custom it is important for everyone to be tactful. To this extent, I disapprove of that kind of missionary righteousness which looks upon deviations from one's own standards as absolutely repugnant. There is a higher way, that of love. This means here that one should try to make others see the *spirit* of one's religion, rather than concentrate upon externals. They can come later.

CB: A properly Buddhist sentiment! It may also be remarked that religion should as far as possible be disengaged from extraneous cultural associations. Christianity and wearing trousers need not go together!

C: Your implied rebuke to some of our missionaries is just. Could we go back to the second point which you made earlier? It's very relevant to this matter of the spirit of religion and morality. You said, as I recall, that a virtue of Buddhism was that it presented a humanitarian ethic free from connection with speculations about God's nature. The Theravāda teaches us a lesson in this. For some of our Christian apologists keep saying that you can't have morality without religion, and religion here means belief in and worship of God. Now Buddhism doesn't necessarily involve this and yet displays a profoundly moral attitude to the world. So our apologists will, I suspect, have to think again. Nevertheless, the spirit of Theravādin morality can't be dissociated from Buddhist ideas of salvation, can it?

CB: No indeed. For instance, certain particular rules are closely connected with our beliefs and spiritual aims. Thus the prohibition on killing fits in with the doctrine of rebirth, and is as well conducive to that serenity of spirit which is the goal of the *arhat*. Then again the ban on drugs and intoxicants goes with our ideal of mindfulness (of gaining clarity of mind and self-control) which is part of the training involved in the Path. But more generally, Buddhist compassion is impregnated with the recognition of the universality of suffering. The diagnosis of the causes of suffering is itself kindly, and not tainted with hate or bitter condemnation: men are foolish or blind, but not precisely *wicked*, in being in the grip of lust and craving. Emphasis upon sin can be dangerous, for then man can adopt an attitude of righteous indignation which only serves to cover his ignorance of his own motives.

J: Nevertheless, once one does conceive of an All-Holy God, one cannot fail to be struck by men's inadequacies, and these blemishes will be seen as sins against God. This is a further illustration of the way in which our views about men, about this world and about the right ideals are influenced by our beliefs about God. The fear of the Lord is the beginning of wisdom.

C: But *only* the beginning! We later see that God is Love. And so, on the human level, righteous indignation gives way to love. And yet, emphasis on sin brings home men's *responsibility*, and this is in our concept of free will.

M: Is there a strong connection here? I think not. We Muslims recognize men's sinfulness; but at the same time all is due to Allah, who even leads men astray. The affirmation of free will in your sense involves a certain dualism: it takes away from God His omnipotence and omnipresence.

C: I can see that this doctrine harmonizes well with the overwhelming insistence on the power and majesty of God so well expressed in the Qu'rān. But this sentiment, though undoubtedly compelling for monotheists, is nevertheless to be set against our ordinary views about moral action. Moral insight, we believe, is itself a kind of insight into divine Truth, and so its deliverances need to be respected. A correct balance is perhaps precarious: but surely it needs to be struck. And it seems to make nonsense of the divine goodness that God should cause our evil acts as well as good ones.

M: Yet although God is cause of everything, man does somehow (on our view) acquire responsibility for his acts. It's perhaps inappropriate here to indulge in subtle discussions of these philosophical and theological issues; for in any case I will concede that pre-destination does create intellectual problems for us. But this is not too high a price to pay for a radical and consistent doctrine of God's nature.

C: And I for my part will agree that my earlier claim as to the connection between sin and freedom of the will wasn't as evident as I thought. But perhaps in these disputes we've moved too far from our original purpose. Originally we set out to discuss the nature of evil in the world, and thereby we got involved in a discussion of God's goodness (and possible badness). From there we turned to a consideration of the relation between faith and practical morality, but we'd not long been embarked on this when we were caught up again in a discusssion of sin *versus* ignorance. But perhaps all this has been a bit theoretical, and we haven't got down to brass tacks. What about the real fruits of faith? What about the goodness which religions have inspired? Aren't these matters relevant to religious truth?

CB: But what are the standards of goodness? Isn't it the case that our evaluations of the fruits of faith will partly depend upon our ideals and upon what we regard as true happiness? Moreover, do we have the facts at our disposal? Millions of lives have been lived in different conditions, of which we know very little. Only someone very close to omniscience (someone perhaps like the Buddha) would know the answers.

M: But we don't need to be so agnostic as you suggest. For instance, we can point not merely to the explosive impact of Islam upon the world in the centuries after Muḥammad, but also to the marvellous brotherhood promoted by our religion.

J: While I can recognize the impact of Islam and even perhaps the brotherhood you mention, nevertheless I feel bound to protest against one aspect of Muslim practical morality. The Prophet is set up as an ideal (and is even, in later thought, regarded as sinless): but while I have a certain respect for him, he doesn't seem to me the best person to imitate. He was war-like and a clever organizer, but though such qualities may be useful among rulers of men, they don't represent the highest ideal, and Muhammad's teachings have inspired quite a lot of bloodshed and rapacity.

M: You're not being fair. Of course it's true that Islam has expanded largely by conquest. But first, as you pointed out earlier, a religion represents a social structure, and the creation of a new society can't be achieved without the use of force. Second, Islam has brought great benefits in religion and culture to the nations which it has dominated. Besides, in any case, you exaggerate the forcefulness of Islam. Our faith wouldn't have conquered so many peoples so rapidly if it hadn't been welcome to the populations concerned. And haven't Jews and Christians fought for their religion? A *jihād* and a Crusade aren't far apart!

H: Hinduism and Buddhism have been pretty peaceable, on the other hand. This has, I've no doubt, something to do with the ideal of *ahiṁsā*.

M: This was a point to which I was coming. Perhaps indeed I should have intervened earlier when you were talking about it. For both in Christianity and in Buddhism we find this deprecation of violence (even if the adherents of these religions have often enough been violent). It's easy to say: 'What a wonderful ideal!' But the wisdom of God is greater than our sentimental ideas: we find in practice that men have no hope of living up to such an ideal of turning the other cheek. It doesn't work and it couldn't work. Of course, one should be gentle and fair in dealing with others. But it's absurd to condemn all bloodshed and all violence. The Christians have recognized this, and thus refute their own Gospel. Thus we can see that though there's something superficially attractive in non-violence, it's at bottom absurd and unworkable. This is a sign that the teachings of the Qu'rān display God's wisdom and helpful instruction for men. As for the application of *ahiṁsā* to animals, I know that it's partly bound up with rebirth doctrine, which we've already agreed to differ about. Apart, however, from this it seems absurd to refuse to take life simply because it is life. If we kill fleas with DDT, why not eat beef? One can see from all this that Islam presents a consistent and wise system of moral teachings, adaptable to human nature and human conditions. In any case, as to the relative bellicosity of different nations and religions, it's hard (if we're thinking of the empirical facts) to make generalizations.

C: On this last point, agreed. But I certainly demur regarding ideals. Of course men are sinful and unsatisfactory, but they must try to rise above it. But when I originally spoke about the fruits of faith, I wasn't wanting to go too much into generalizations or statistics. I was thinking of the way religions present different moral attitudes and ideals—Christian *agapé*, Buddhist compassion, Jewish righteousness, and so on.

CB: And yet if we turn to ideals, how are we to judge between them? You have implicitly rejected statistics, so now we're discussing the matter in a very woolly way. Moreover, there is the question of practical advice, even apart from the ideals. Here, I suspect, the Theravāda is most helpful; for Buddhism lays down clear methods of training the mind, both in respect of insight and in respect of moral goodness. There are different exercises in meditation which are both helpful and easy to grasp, even if they are often difficult to perform. For instance, one mentally divides the world into four quarters and then meditates on the beings in each quarter in turn, suffusing them with love. This kind of exercise is practical and owes nothing to speculative theories. Some kinds of religion, relying on faith and on God's grace, seem to give an exalted picture of God's nature, but do they provide the practical teaching which is necessary for self-improvement.

M: Islam lays down clear rules of conduct. So does Judaism and, to some extent, Christianity.

CB: Yes, but as to changing men's hearts, is there a comparable system of training to that found on Buddhism?

C: Perhaps we haven't stressed psychological training as much as we might have done; but the transforming work is in the end done by God, and it's not a thing to be contrived by man on his own. This is where we clash again, simply because we hold different views about eternity.

JB: The Pure Land sect, as represented by the teachings of Hōnen, propounds views about faith and works of an undeniably theistic character. It's perhaps an advantage of the Great Vehicle that it is so comprehensive. There are different possibilities open to the adherent: it is not a closed system, but one which is replete with experiment and new developments. And where truth is hard to search out, this is a good thing. For men aren't constricted rigidly to one view. However, it appears to me that we're in danger of going over ground which we've already trodden in this discussion. For it is clear that the various flavours and emphases in the respective moral attitudes of our different faiths do trace back to different views about the world. Hence, we can't go much further without reverting to our earlier disagreements and agreements about doctrines. On the other hand, I think we have done well to repudiate statistics, since it is well-nigh impossible to judge between the multifarious practical effects of our different religions. Here one can only judge through personal acquaintance with the different societies and individuals. Even here it's difficult to disentangle that which is due to religion from that which is due to the inherent qualities of particular societies and individuals.

C: Perhaps this rather inconclusive result is a good thing. For although we've seen (in regard, for instance, to the Muslim view on what constitutes *practical* teaching as to morality) that a religious doctrine may be recommended in that it chimes in with our moral views or may be viewed as unsatisfactory where it does not express a deep enough insight into morality, yet the main tendency is in the opposite direction. For our diagnoses of men's troubles are closely linked to our beliefs about the cosmos and what lies beyond the cosmos. Moreover, as religious people we come to look upon moral action in a special way: for the theist it is looked upon as a way of serving and worshipping God, and for the Theravādin as a part of the spiritual training culminating in peace and insight. Further, the question: 'Are people morally better because of religion?' does seem to me to be an unreal one. The relevant question would have to be: 'Would I be better if I believed?' But clearly one should not believe in something just because it would make one better, but because it is *true*. Therefore the prior question must be as to the truth of religion. In other words, it was our earlier discussion, about doctrines, which was the important one; and therefore our rather inconclusive consideration of moral differences is, fortunately, not in any fatal way inconclusive. Perhaps we can agree that while religion is vastly important in its bearing upon morality, since it provides (as it were) the cosmic framework for action and suffuses daily life with a certain spirit, it is impossible to establish the truth of religion simply by reference to moral insight.

J: Nevertheless, you did say (and I agree with you) that moral insight is itself a kind of insight into the divine Truth.

C: Yes, though it is also clear from our discussion that it is difficult to see in detail how such insight affects our views about ultimate Reality. It is perhaps again, as with our disagreements about the relation between the numinous and the mystical, partly a matter of *emphasis*. Christianity, for example, may be commended because its realism about the material world, illuminated by the Incarnation, itself helps to give a prominent place to moral insight. Moral action is important in a real world in which both good and evil are to be found. Again, the Mahāyāna criticism of the Theravāda, as I understand it, turns on the point that excessive concentration upon the goal of release causes compassion to take second place to a higher prudence. In addition to this, however, there are divergences about the moral insight itself. As we have seen, Islam is strongly practical in its bent: and therefore thinks that a supposed ideal which can't work in practice cannot represent a genuine moral insight. (Some of the Ṣūfīs, however, influenced by the thought of union with God as love, have come nearer to the Christian and Buddhist standpoint.) No doubt there could be a lengthy discussion of such differences within morality itself. But perhaps enough has been said to sketch the kinds of consideration which we take into account. In any case, the main point still stands, namely that it is wiser to start with religious truth itself, rather than to start at the moral end. To this extent, our earlier discussion of doctrines is of prior importance.

CB: In that case, could you then round off our little conference by summing up such agreements and disagreements about doctrines as we have come to?

C: Certainly. I shall try.

VIII

CONCLUSION

C: At the beginning of our discussion we agreed that, other things being equal, monotheism is superior to polytheism. We did not, however, exclude the possibility that monism would be a better account of Ultimate Reality than monotheism. We recognized, in regard to both monotheism and monism, that these have the (admittedly rather *formal* advantage) of being simpler doctrines than polytheism. In addition, it was felt that some of the overwhelming numinous experiences of prophets and saints point in the direction of one God, rather than in the direction of many 'this-worldly' deities: in comparison with such theophanies, the idea of the many gods of mythology seems blasphemous. This, however, led to the question of which was the right way to treat polytheism. On this there was some disagreement. On the one hand, the Judaic group of faiths condemn polytheism with varying degrees of violence. But there is a different view elsewhere. The Theravāda allows that there may be gods, but assigns them little importance. The Mahāyāna incorporates something very like gods (the Bodhisattvas and celestial Buddhas). And Hinduism not only recognizes different levels of spiritual enlightenment, but treats them in an 'educational' way. How to choose between these different attitudes? In the Judaic faiths, the stern condemnation of polytheism (even if angels aren't excluded!) stems from the burning vision of one Lord. (And we recognized in passing that from the Jewish and Muslim point of view there is apparent polytheism in Christianity; but Christians have defended the Trinity through the doctrine that there is only one substance, though different Persons). Also we noted that the greater degree of 'agnosticism' in Hinduism and Buddhism lends itself to a more tolerant view of doctrines. On the other hand, it can be argued that this leads to dangerous compromise.

It was at this point suggested that the 'educational' theory in Hinduism is not unconnected with the doctrines of reincarnation and rebirth—a major point of divergence between the Indian and Middle Eastern religions. Here, doubtless, empirical evidence becomes relevant (an advantage and a danger for any doctrine!). But though there is divergence on this issue, it doesn't imply that Eastern notions of salvation are so very different from, say, Christian ones: the difference largely lies in what it is salvation *from*. And *mokṣa* and *nirvāṇa* may well correspond to the attainments of Christian, Jewish and Muslim contemplatives. At the same time, there is not, in the Theravāda, immortality in any straightforward sense (for the Buddha condemned speculations about the eternity of the self), even though *nirvāṇa* is described as a deathless place. Again, whereas Christian conceptions of immortality (ignoring the doctrine of the Resurrection of the Body) and their analogues (especially in Islam) involve personal and distinct survival, not an impersonal merging with the Absolute, the latter idea is found in Advaita Vedānta and in some forms of the Mahāyāna. Also, in our discussion, we noted how the Indian cyclical view of the universe (which is connected with rebirth) contrasts with the 'directional' and historical view of the Judaic group. Both the 'impersonalism' sometimes found in Indian religion and this unhistorical approach trace back to, or harmonize with, different conceptions of God (save in the Theravāda, about which more below). It was therefore necessary for us to go on to discuss the reasons for divergence about ultimate Reality.

Here the Theravāda necessarily intruded into our discussion, seeing that here there is no doctrine of God. How can it be that what is undoubtedly a religion (for it leads to salvation and involves spiritual meditative practices) has no belief in God? The question is acute where we find resemblances between Buddhist mysticism and theistic mysticism (external resemblances, even if they are not absolute correspondences in terms of descriptions). It was suggested that there are loose analogies between things said about *nirvāṇa* and things said about God. These analogies, while loose enough on the one hand to make it perfectly intelligible to have mysticism without belief in God, are suggestive enough to make a theistic interpretation not entirely out of the question.

It was not, however, suggested that a theistic interpretation was possible in the sense that one might say that the Buddha was really preaching a crypto-theism; but only in the sense that the experiences involved in the Eightfold Path, in going to the 'Other Shore', might themselves be given a theistic interpretation. *Might* be, not necessarily *should* be.

It was pointed out that whereas a theistic interpretation would weld together the insights of contemplation and those of worship (the insights respectively of the numinous and the mystical), the Theravāda teachings were undoubtedly simpler than such a complex interpretation. Thus the Hindu schools which (in varying ways) associate the Brahman with the Ātman, Mahāyānists, the Ṣūfīs, the Jewish and Christian mystics—all these are saying something more complicated than that which was said (according to the Theravāda) by the Buddha. His teachings had a beautiful minimal simplicity, just as conversely the teachings of early Islam have a simplicity of another sort (a simple, majestic concept of the Object of Worship). It was then asked how we should balance richness (with its attendant complexity) against simplicity. No very helpful answer was given here—though, for what it is worth, there is the historical lesson that just as Islam developed its mystical side, so Buddhism, in the Great Vehicle, developed its numinous side. On the other hand, it was noted that the identification of the Object of Worship with the mystical goal leads to tensions, and is, in its complication, hazardous. But it is worth noting at this point that in our discussions we weren't pretending to describe how one would, so to speak, make up revelations from scratch: indeed such an idea seems blasphemous and inappropriate (we are not prophets or teachers). The different revelations and doctrinal schemes are 'given'; and it has been our task merely to see how different aspects of them hang together.

These matters brought us to a discussion of monism versus monotheism. It was suggested that the emphasis on a rather 'impersonal' view of the Absolute, where It is described in terms of Being and other such ontological expressions, chimes in with mystical insight, in the sense that the interior vision has no ordinary descriptive content, and so such abstract terms have a use here. On the other hand, the numinous being lying behind the cosmos and who is the object of worship is characteristically described in a personalistic manner. Thus the Advaita scale of values, whereby the Lord is merely a lower manifestation of the Absolute, perhaps represents a greater emphasis on *gnosis* or mystical *vidyā* than on anything else. Its monistic character in identifying Brahman and Ātman reflects the lack of the subject-object distinction in the interior vision. On the other hand, theistic mystics often preserve the difference between God and man which is required by the whole spirit of worship and devotion by interpreting the relationship in terms of love and spiritual marriage, etc. In this way, they can reconcile union and devotion: for in marriage there is a 'two who are yet one'. This devotional side to theistic mysticism makes the atmosphere of their quest rather different from that of the monistic or agnostic contemplative; and perhaps this difference of atmosphere suffuses the experience itself.

In defence of the monistic impersonalism, it was pointed out that worship itself transcends anthropomorphism: it transcends ordinary descriptions of God, for we get to the stage of thinking that God is not as we conceive Him—He is majestically more. And in addition some of his attributes (like creativity) are related to the contingent cosmos and so are not (so to speak) part of His essence. For such reasons, it seems to be part of the logic of worship that it should transcend itself. On the other hand, the Advaitin system of priorities will not commend itself to those who regard themselves (directly or through their own tradition) as having had the shattering revelation of a Personal Being who calls forth our worship and obedience. Moreover, there was the argument mentioned that whereas putting mystical insight prior to the experience of a personal object of worship tends to mean that the latter is, so to speak, swallowed up, the converse does not hold. As has been said: 'If the worshipper and the object of worship are one, how can there be any worship?' We also noticed a similar emphasis in some Mahāyāna teachings to that found in the Advaita, in that in worshipping the Tathāgata one is adoring one's own ultimate state. There was a further consideration relevant to Christians in particular (and also to Vaiṣṇavite Hindus and others), namely that a doctrine of incarnation seems to imply the personalistic view of God.

But before going on to discuss the Christian belief in the Incarnation, we had a look at the Three-Body doctrine in the Mahāyāna, with its at least superficial resemblance to the Trinity doctrine. We saw that the spirit of Buddhist teachings here often bears a remarkable likeness to that of Christianity (the Bodhisattva ideal, compassion or love, the merit that can be conveyed to the faithful by Buddhas-to-be, the promise of heaven, and so on). Nevertheless, though the Buddha in his Transformation-Body looks like an incarnation, there is a tendency to docetism in the Buddhist picture. Further, strict monotheists, as are found in the Judaic group, would object to the multiplication of celestial Buddhas, as being polytheistic in appearance. To this it was replied that Buddhism is ultimately monistic, since the Buddhas are all united in the Truth-Body or in the Absolute. But here we reverted to the old collision between monotheism and monism, and the system of priorities again. Also we harked back to the not unconnected dispute about how polytheism (or apparent polytheism) should be viewed: should it be rigidly excluded or treated imaginatively and educationally? In addition, the rigidly monotheistic view of Islam considers that any notion of incarnation or Tathāgata-ship is blasphemous, as being out of accord with the majestic nature of God and with the injunction to repudiate other gods and graven images.

However, the comparison of the Mahāyāna with Christianity naturally focused our attention upon the respective historicity of the two lots of doctrines. For Christians rely upon historical evidence much more explicitly and firmly. But it was necessary first to consider the Gandhian objection to the exclusiveness of Christianity and the general Eastern feelings that if there be human manifestations of the Deity there is no compulsion to believe in just *one* such manifestation. Here we had to balance the scandalous particularity of Christianity against the 'messiness' (and blasphemy, from one point of view) of multiple incarnations. Connectedly, the Christian belief has the formal merit of simplicity. More importantly, there is the Christian claim that Christ is Saviour; and the logic of this implies that He is fully man as well as God. Hence the Christian objection to docetism; and there is a tendency in this direction in beliefs in multiple incarnations. Moreover, we had seen that the 'dualism' involved in the religion of worship and devotion involves a realism about the creature and creation, whereas the impersonalistic view of the Absolute (in line with the contemplative's detachment from the world) may issue in a feeling of the unreality of the phenomenal world. Thus Absolutism and docetism may tend to go together.

On the other hand, with regard to multiplicity of incarnations, modern biological and astronomical discoveries do not exclude the hypothesis that there are rational creatures elsewhere in the cosmos. While this, together with the incredible vastness of the universe, squares with Buddhist and Hindu imagery, it may be embarrassing for Christians, since it might seem to imply that God will have become incarnate elsewhere— and this takes the edge off Christian criticisms of the Hindu conception of *avatāras*, etc.; though the Christian doctrine remains the simplest we know, and is the doctrine most consonant with rigid monotheism.

It was, however, pointed out that the Christian claim rests above all on historical evidence, although we agreed that something more than this was required. For this reason, we spoke together about the 'criteria' of divinity, so far as they could be perceived, and the nature of evidence about Christ. Herein some stress was laid on Christ's role as Saviour, and it was therefore natural to go on to say something about the evil from which we are supposed to be delivered.

About this there was disagreement between us, which can be crudely summed up by contrasting Original Sin with 'Original Ignorance'. This contrast arises at least in part from different conceptions of ultimate Reality. For where the emphasis is upon mystical *gnosis*, salvation tends to be in terms of insight, with which is contrasted our ordinary ignorance. Where on the other hand, the stress is on the religion of worship and devotion, with its attendant dualism between worshipper and Object of Worship, we will tend to speak of deliverance from sin (as being the converse of holiness—for the Supreme Being is here conceived as all-holy). Some objection was taken, in this connection, to the story of the Fall, though I tried to show how it harmonized with theism in being 'analogical history'.

Inasmuch as there was thought to be some connection between the notion of God as 'beyond good and evil' and the contemplative quest (for it usually involves withdrawal from society, as well as having an 'agnostic' bias), we turned our attention to the practical aspects of the various moralities enshrined in religions. Unfortunately this led us to begin making crude generalizations about our relative merits, and so we decided to abandon a fruitless search for statistics, but agreed at least that there is some connection in spirit between a system of doctrine and the associated code of morality. Doubtless we can see how different beliefs illuminate and comprehend morality in different ways. However, though our conclusions were somewhat sketchy, this was accounted no great loss, since the *prior* question must be the truth of doctrine, before we can decide which is the best morality for us. It might be thought that the main point of religion is to make us live better, but how can one understand what 'better' means without recourse to the idea of ultimate well-being? And how can this be understood without trying to find the truth about God and the cosmos?

These, then, were, I think, the main points which we agreed or disagreed upon.

H: A fair recapitulation; but it leaves us rather perplexed as to what the most important principles are.

C: I suspect that although there are disagreements enough between us, nevertheless our discussion has been *relevant*. And relevance should imply that we can do something to sketch the principles of argument. First, we have sometimes appealed to the rather formal principle of simplicity (other things being equal). Second, we have appealed to two different sorts of religious experience, the numinous and the mystical (this of course is a distinction which we've had to make in a rather crude manner), and this raises the question of whether there are analogies between the two. So another principle is that we may justify association through appeal to something like aesthetic analogies. That is, one who sees in the contemplatives' goal a union with the Object of Worship may make his doctrine reasonable, and perhaps acceptable, through such appeals. But here we have the difficult task of balancing richness against simplicity. Third, the elucidation of such aesthetic analogies involves the explication of what may be called the 'inner logic' of religious experience—how holiness contrasts with sin, in the numinous strand of experience; how the subject-object relationship seems to vanish in the mystical experience; and so on. This 'inner logic' helps us to see how things hang together in one cluster of doctrines; but also it leads to tensions, where there is an intertwining of different strands of doctrine. Thus, for example, we have seen how a belief in the Incarnation must, *prima facie*, be regarded as blasphemous by the monotheist. This bears on the theistic attitude to polytheism also. Fourth, we saw how the 'inner logic' of experience has an effect outside doctrines about the ultimate or transcendent Reality, for it partly controls attitudes to the world. Thus, we saw that the dualism of worshipper and Object of Worship tends towards realism, and the monism of the mystical experience reflects itself in an idealistic attitude to the empirical world. Again, notions about sin and ignorance reflect different emphases in regard to the numinous and the mystical. Fifth, we observed that there are different ways of blending these elements in experience, though we weren't clear as to how the scale of values is to be determined. Perhaps this partly depends upon what can be called 'intensity' of experience. Finally, of course, we saw that in some contexts (e.g. the story of the Fall as literally interpreted, belief in rebirth, and the historicity of Christ) empirical evidence is relevant, though perhaps not in all cases decisive. These aren't the only principles we came across, but they do give a rough outline of the ways in which we were arguing.

H: An admirable survey, though you perhaps should have mentioned the uneasiness expressed by some of us at the *particularity* of the Judaic faiths, especially Christianity. But let us not repeat our arguments about that. I was reminded, while you were speaking, of discussions one sometimes has about art or music. Often there we can adumbrate principles of relevance in a somewhat murky manner; and yet agreement is not easily arrived at. One needs insight and receptivity. I believe the same is true of religion: our criteria are 'soft' rather than 'hard'; and there don't seem to be any knock-down arguments. We are, so to speak, between the rational and the non-rational. Yet some may think that there's a paradox here. For isn't religious insight supposed to yield certainty? Does our discussion mean that we can't have it?

C: I think our discussion *does* show that a degree of tolerance in doctrinal manners is desirable. But as for *certainty*, well, perhaps there's a kind of personal assurance we can have, even if there's no set of cut-and-dried public criteria which would bring us to an absolutely definite and generally accepted set of conclusions. But what do people expect? Do they expect literally to see God? Is *nirvāṇa* something that can be photographed? If God appeared in that way, He would, I suspect, so overwhelm us as to deprive us of freedom and the possibility of loving Him. There surely must be mystery in these matters. Doctrines, to this extent, must be regarded as tentative: the way in which we clothe the Truth is tentative.

M: Is it? But Allah has . . .

H: I hate to interrupt, but I can see what you're going to say. Please do not say it now, for I'd hate us to end on such a note of radical disagreement. We have had disagreements enough, though happily they have been friendly ones. But if we were to agree that the criteria are 'soft' this would support a secret thought of mine: the thought that our argument has led to a rather Hindu conclusion.

C: Perhaps. But since revelations and teachings are 'given', and we don't think them up of our own accord, I suppose that your remark could be misinterpreted. Still, it would be a conciliatory note to end on, and you've half persuaded me to look upon doctrines in a more Hindu way. But I give notice that however Hindu I may be, I shall remain a Hindu Christian!

JB: What more could he ask?

GLOSSARY

(Where a word or name appears in capitals, this indicates that it has a separate entry in the glossary)

ADVAITA VEDĀNTA Non-dualistic VEDĀNTA, perhaps the most influential interpretation of the Hindu scriptures, systematized by ŚAṄKARA. It is 'non-dualistic', because it asserts that there is only one Reality and because there is no dualism between the ĀTMAN and BRAHMAN. Often 'Advaita' is used by itself to refer to Advaita Vedānta.

ADVAITIN Pertaining to, or an adherent of, the ADVAITA VEDĀNTA.

AHIṂSĀ Non-violence. This teaching, specially prominent in Buddhism and JAINISM, proscribes the taking of life and inculcates a gentle attitude to all living creatures.

AMITĀBHA One of the best-known Buddhas of devotional Buddhism, who has created a paradise (the Pure Land far to the West) into which those who call upon his name with faith will be reborn.

ANATTĀ This is the PĀLI form of the Sanskrit *anātman*, i.e. non-ĀTMAN. The Buddha's doctrine of *anattā* is that there is no Self or ĀTMAN either in the cosmos or in individuals: there is no permanent underlying Self behind psychological phenomena, but a person is simply a stream of impermanent states, experiences, etc. *Anattā* is, with ANICCA and DUKKHA, one of the three characteristics of all individual existence.

ANICCA 'Impermanent' (PĀLI). The Buddha's teaching is that all things are impermanent, a constant succession of changes, with nothing permanent underlying them. (However, this view is modified in the MAHĀYĀNA with the elaboration of the concept of an Absolute: see also DHARMAKĀYA.)

ARHAT Literally 'worthy one'. Name used for a Buddhist saint, i.e. one who has attained NIRVĀṆA. The *arhat* ideal, of the liberated contemplative, gave way, in the MAHĀYĀNA, to a broader view of the path to salvation and to emphasis on the ideal of the BODHISATTVA.

ĀTMAN The Self or soul, the eternal aspect of a living being. In ŚAṄKARA's system the Self is identified with BRAHMAN, the one Reality, and so there is truly only one Self. Other Hindu theologians differ from Śaṅkara and, in varying ways, postulate a plurality of souls. See, for example, SĀṄKHYA.

AVATAR   See AVATĀRA.

AVATĀRA   'Descent' or, more loosely, 'incarnation' of God upon earth. See also KRISHNA, VIṢṆU.

AVIDYĀ   'Ignorance', i.e. lack of VIDYĀ, lack of metaphysical or spiritual insight. In the ADVAITA, the cosmos, looked at from one point of view as MĀYĀ, is also the product of Ignorance—for we take the world to be real because we are ignorant of the higher truth that there is only one Reality, namely BRAHMAN-ĀTMAN.

BHAGAVADGĪTĀ   Song (Gītā) of the Lord (Bhagavad), perhaps the most famous religious writing of Hinduism. It constitutes one book of the vast Indian epic poem, the Mahābhārata, and was probably written in its present form before the Birth of Christ (though scholars differ about this). It presents a synthesis of ideas derived from BHAKTI religion, the teachings of the UPANIṢADS and those of SĀṄKHYA-YOGA.

BHAKTI   'Loving adoration'. 'Bhakti religion' is a name given to the religion of faith in a personal Lord (ĪŚVARA) which developed strongly in Hinduism after the period of the early UPANIṢADS. One can also speak of bhakti in Buddhism, etc., i.e. wherever there is the attitude of loving adoration.

BHIKKHU   The PĀLI word for 'mendicant', i.e. Buddhist monk.

BODHI   Buddhist Enlightenment, the profound insight and illumination attained by a BUDDHA.

BODHISATTVA   Buddha-to-be, i.e. someone destined for BODHI. The conception is central to the MAHĀYĀNA, with its stress upon compassion. The Bodhisattva, in his many lives leading up to the final enlightenment, stores up so much merit, through his sacrifices on behalf of living beings, that he may transfer such merit to other less worthy beings. They thereby may be assisted on the road to Paradise and to NIRVĀṆA.

BRAHMĀ   The personal creator God in Hinduism. Together with ŚIVA and VIṢṆU he forms the classical Hindu 'trinity'.

BRAHMAN   This neuter word is used in the UPANIṢADS and elsewhere for the Sacred Power sustaining the cosmos. The sacred power, brahman, originally stood for the power implicit in the sacrificial ritual which played a large part in VEDIC religion, and behind the more general notion is the hint that things are 'kept going' by the sacrificial ritual. In the ADVAITA VEDĀNTA, Brahman is identified with the ĀTMAN.

BUDDHA   Enlightened One. See also TRIKĀYA.

BUDDHAGHOSA   Distinguished THERAVĀDIN monk, of the 5th century A D, who wrote extensive commentaries on the PĀLI canon and who was the author of the VISUDDHIMAGGA or PATH OF PURITY, which is perhaps the best summary that there is of the Buddhist Path as it is conceived in the THERAVĀDA.

CIT   Consciousness. The word is sometimes used for the ĀTMAN, which can be looked on as pure consciousness.

DHAMMA   The PĀLI form of the Sanskrit DHARMA. It is used especially for the Buddha's teaching. Thus when the Buddhist says 'I take refuge in the Dhamma', he is taking refuge in the Teaching.

DHARMA   'Religion', 'law', 'truth'. In Hinduism, *dharma*, considered at the social level, comprises the duties in life which one's position and circumstances impose upon one. This includes both religious and moral duties, custom, etc. Thus the Hindu word for the whole complex of that which controls life is *dharma*, and is therefore the nearest equivalent to our word 'religion'.

DHARMAKĀYA   Truth-Body. See TRIKĀYA.

DUKKHA   Suffering, painfulness. According to the Buddhist teaching, all life is characterized by suffering, the cure for this being the attainment of NIRVĀNA. See ANATTĀ.

EIGHTFOLD PATH   The Noble Eightfold Path sums up the Buddha's prescription on how to attain NIRVĀNA. The first two 'stages' of the Path, Right View and Right Aspiration, refer to the attitude to be taken up by the aspirant for *nirvāna*; the next three, Right Speech, Right Conduct and Right Means of Livelihood, refer to the moral and social requirements to be met by the aspirant; while the last three, Right Endeavour, Right Mindfulness (SATI) and Right Contemplation, refer to the mental and spiritual disciplines that are needed.

GREAT VEHICLE   See MAHĀYĀNA.

HŌNEN 12th-century Japanese saint and exponent of JŌDO piety, which stresses the need to call on the name of the Buddha AMITĀBHA.

ĪŚVARA Lord. This term is the one most frequently used for God as a person, or for the personal aspect of the Godhead.

JAINISM The religion associated with Mahāvīra, a contemporary of Gautama the Buddha. It has similarities both to SĀṄKHYA and to Buddhism; but unlike the former it is unorthodox from the Hindu point of view, since it does not recognize the Hindu scriptures, and unlike the latter it has not had any wide missionary success. The term 'Jainism' derives from the word *jina* or 'conqueror', a title given to Mahāvīra (and also sometimes to the Buddha). The Jain community in contemporary India is more influential than its numbers would suggest, since Jains have been long established in merchant and business activities, partly because a rigid insistence on AHIṀSĀ makes it impossible for the loyal Jain to follow occupations such as farming or soldiering, which involve the taking of life.

JAMBUDVĪPA Sanskrit term for the Indian sub-continent.

JHĀNA Meditation. The *jhānas* are the central stages of Buddhist meditation, culminating in the stage where the contemplative passes beyond the sphere of ordinary perceptions.

JIHĀD The duty enjoined in the Qu'rān, ii. 186 f., to fight 'in the way of God' against those who attack Islam. The conception of a Holy War has, however, largely fallen into disuse in contemporary Islam.

JŌDO Japanese term for the Pure Land School. The Jōdo Shin Shū, i.e. True Pure Land School, founded by Shinran, a Japanese teacher of the 12th-13th centuries A D, who had been influenced by HŌNEN, is the largest of the Japanese Buddhist sects. Shinran went beyond Hōnen's pietistic teachings in giving up the monastic and celibate life, inasmuch as it suggests that salvation can be achieved by 'works'.

KĀLĪ Consort of ŚIVA. She is his female counterpart and symbolizes the projected energy of the Divine Being.

KARMA Literally 'deed' or 'action'. The law of *karma* determines a person's status in the round of rebirth or reincarnation (SAṀSĀRA) in accordance with his deeds in past lives.

KARUṆĀ Compassion. Loving compassion is the central Buddhist virtue, and is very strongly emphasized in the teachings of the MAHĀYĀNA, especially in connection with the BODHISATTVA ideal.

KRISHNA Sanskrit Kṛṣṇa. An AVATĀRA of VIṢṆU, around whom many legends cluster concerning Krishna's rural boyhood among the cowherds and his prowess as an ideal warrior-king (probably two lines of tradition have become mingled here).

LESSER VEHICLE See THERAVĀDA.

MĀDHYAMIKA Influential philosophical school of the MAHĀYĀNA founded by Nāgārjuna, *c.* A D 200. It involves a subtle dialectic which shows that all extremes, i.e. all statements together with their contradictories, concerning reality are self-contradictory. All empirical phenomena are relative and thus void of reality, but although this drives one to think in terms of an Absolute underlying phenomena, this itself cannot be consistently spoken of, but must simply be referred to as the Void (ŚŪNYA).

MAHĀYĀNA The Great Vehicle, in contradistinction to the Hīnayāna or LESSER VEHICLE. The idea is that the Mahāyāna is a broad path to salvation, as opposed to the supposed narrowness of the Lesser Vehicle with its concentration on the ARHAT ideal. Through the conception of BODHISATTVAS and celestial Buddhas (see TRIKĀYA), there developed the teaching that men can, through faith in the Buddha, attain to a state of heavenly bliss (see JŌDO, PURE LAND) and finally thus to NIRVĀṆA without undergoing the more strenuous and 'introvert' discipline of the aspiring ARHAT.

MĀYĀ The magical power displayed by the Creator (ĪSVARA) in the ADVAITA VEDĀNTA. *Māyā* has the suggestion of 'illusion' in it, so that the empirical cosmos, the *māyā* of God, is unreal —there being only one Reality, BRAHMAN-ĀTMAN.

MĀRA The chief Evil Spirit in Buddhism, sometimes standing for evil psychological tendencies in man. Māra is said to have tempted the Buddha when he sat alone under the Bo Tree about to gain Enlightenment. The Buddha triumphed over the Tempter.

MOKṢA 'Liberation', 'release'—usually conceived, in Indian religion, as liberation from SAṀSĀRA.

NEMBUTSU (Japanese) 'calling on the name of the Buddha', the repetition of a formula expressing loving faith in the Buddha AMITĀBHA which plays a central part in JŌDO piety.

NIBBĀNA Pāli form of the word NIRVĀṆA.

NIRGUṆAM Without attributes. In higher truth, according to the ADVAITA VEDĀNTA, BRAHMAN is *nirguṇam*, without attributes or qualifications, and so is contrasted with the Brahman *with* attributes, the ĪŚVARA or Lord whom those at the stage of lower truth worship and adore.

NIRMĀṆAKĀYA Transformation-Body. See TRIKĀYA.

NIRVĀṆA A word for liberation in Indian religion and in Buddhism in particular. Literally, it means 'the going out', as of a flame—the point being that it is the flame of desire or craving (see TAṆHĀ) which causes rebirth, and therefore the extinction of craving will bring about liberation from SAṀSĀRA. There is a distinction between *nirvāṇa* with and without substrate. When a saint attains *nirvāṇa* in this life, he will not be reborn, but still retains his 'substrate', i.e. his body and other empirical characteristics. At death he attains *nirvāṇa* without substrate—all his empirical characteristics having disappeared. It is then inappropriate to regard him either as existent or non-existent. *Nirvāṇa* in this life involves gaining supreme serenity and insight, thus dispelling craving and ignorance.

PĀLI The language of the scriptures of the THERAVĀDA; it is fairly closely related to Sanskrit.

PATH OF PURITY This is the English title of the VISUDDHIMAGGA, a book written by BUDDHAGHOSA. It contains a valuable account of THERAVĀDIN meditative practices.

PURE LAND A Buddhist paradise. The Pure Land School of Buddhism, which has been particularly popular in China and Japan (see JŌDO), teaches devotion to celestial Buddha and notably AMITĀBHA, who has prepared a paradise (the Pure Land far to the West) whither, through calling on the name of the Buddha in faith, one will be translated upon death.

RĀMĀNUJA Famous Hindu theologian, AD 1175–1250, who opposed ŚANKARA's uncompromising non-dualism and formulated the *viśiṣṭādvaita* or 'qualified non-dualism', in which he stressed the personal nature of God (Rāmānuja was a VAIṢṆAVITE), the need of BHAKTI and the separate nature of human souls.

SAMBHOGAKĀYA Enjoyment- or Bliss-Body. See TRIKĀYA.

ŚANKARA Famous Hindu theologian, born *c.* AD 788, who systematized the teachings of the ADVAITA VEDĀNTA.

SĀNKHYA One of the traditional systems of Indian metaphysics, closely associated with YOGA. Its main teachings are as follows. (1) There is a fundamental distinction between matter (*prakṛti*) and soul (*puruṣa*); (2) there are innumerable souls, and these are involved in matter and therefore with the endless round of SAṀSĀRA; (3) liberation consists in the individual soul's isolating itself from matter and thereby escaping further entanglement in rebirth; (4) liberation accrues upon insight (*viveka*), whereby the soul perceives its essential distinctness from matter. Yoga adopts the general metaphysical system of Sānkhya, but asserts that liberation requires a certain form of physical and mental discipline.

SANNYĀSIN One who has retired from active life to devote himself to spiritual concerns. This possibility is controlled in Hinduism by the doctrine of four stages of life—that of being a student, that of the householder (i.e. family man), that of one who withdraws from the householder's duties, and finally that of the homeless wanderer or religious mendicant.

SATI The PĀLI word for 'recollection' or 'mindfulness'. Right *sati* figures as one of the last three stages of the EIGHTFOLD PATH. It is a central part of Buddhist mental and spiritual training always to be 'mindful' or 'aware' of what one is doing, one's motives, etc.

ŚIVA One of the two great gods of devotional Hinduism. See VIṢṆU. Śiva is often portrayed as rather terrible, and symbolizes the destructive as well as the creative powers of God, and his consort KĀḶĪ is commonly pictured as peculiarly fierce (wearing a necklace of skulls, etc.). As well as being an object of devotion, Śiva is associated with austerity and contemplation.

ṢŪFĪ The name commonly used for Muslim contemplatives; it probably derives from *ṣūf*, meaning 'wool', the white woollen garment being a badge of penitence. From the 9th century onwards the Ṣūfī movement gained considerable force, though it was not always easy to reconcile the teachings of individual contemplatives with those of orthodox Islam.

ŚŪNYA 'Void', 'empty'. The MĀDHYAMIKA philosophy emphasizes the voidness (ŚŪNYATĀ) of the Absolute, for it cannot be described in empirical terms and all theories or views about it fall into self-contradiction.

ŚŪNYATĀ 'Voidness'; abstract noun from ŚŪNYA, used to characterize the Absolute in certain Mahāyānist teachings.

ŚŪNYAVĀDA The doctrine of the Void, ŚŪNYA.

TAṆHĀ The PĀLI word for 'craving' or 'desire': the cause of rebirth, on the Buddhist view, and itself the product of ignorance. It is thought of as *flaming* or *burning*. See NIRVĀṆA.

TAT TVAM ASI 'That art thou'. This famous saying, found in the UPANIṢADS, expresses the thought that in some sense or other God and the Self are one, i.e. BRAHMAN is ĀTMAN. For the ADVAITA, this is numerical identity; for dualist theologians, it is not identity but similarity.

TATHĀGATA Title used of a Buddha; one who has come (*āgata*) thus (*tathā*), i.e. one who has arrived at a condition which cannot be described, but can only be said to be 'thus' or 'like this'. See TATHATĀ.

TATHATĀ 'Thusness', 'Suchness'—a word used in the MAHĀYĀNA for the Absolute or Ultimate Reality. The use of the word 'Suchness' indicates that it cannot be described in ordinary language. See TRIKĀYA, ŚŪNYA.

THERAVĀDA A PĀLI term, meaning 'Doctrine of the Elders'. This is the name for the school of Buddhism extant in Ceylon, Burma and South-East Asia, and which is often referred to as 'Hīnayāna Buddhism' or 'the LESSER VEHICLE'. Strictly, the THERAVĀDA is only one among the original Hīnayāna schools—the rest having disappeared. Further, there is an objection to using the word 'Hīnayāna', since it was in the first instance used as a term of opprobrium by the opponents of the Hīnayāna. See MAHĀYĀNA.

THERAVĀDIN   Pertaining to, or an adherent of, the THERAVĀDA.

THREE-BODY DOCTRINE   See TRIKĀYA.

TRIKĀYA   The Three-Body doctrine expounded in some Mahāyānist writings. (*Tri*: 'three'; *kāya*: 'body'). According to this
doctrine, the Buddha may be regarded as having three
bodies: (1) the DHARMAKĀYA or Truth-Body, which is
equated with the Absolute; (2) the SAMBHOGAKĀYA or
Enjoyment- (or Bliss-) Body—the form in which the celestial
Buddhas appear (corresponding to the gods of Hinduism);
(3) the NIRMĀNAKĀYA or Transformation-Body—the form in
which the Buddha may manifest himself on earth, as, e.g.,
the historical Gautama Buddha. The Buddhas are sometimes
spoken of as innumerable, but in their Truth-Body they are
all one.

UPANIṢADS   A class of writings belonging to the Hindu scriptures.
They are miscellaneous in character, containing dialogues,
exposition, invocations, etc. Broadly, they seek to give an
account of the inner meaning of traditional (VEDIC) religion.
The most famous Upaniṣads belong roughly to the period
from the 8th to the 5th century B C, though some later works
such as the BHAGAVADGĪTĀ which have been called Upaniṣads have gained a considerable influence as well.

VAIṢṆAVITE   Devotee of VIṢṆU.

VEDA   Literally 'knowledge', i.e. sacred knowledge: a word used
for the early scriptures of Hinduism, consisting in the first
instance of collections of hymns (the Vedas) to which were
added accounts of the rituals, etc., to which in turn were
added expositions of the inner meaning of religious acts, the
UPANIṢADS.

VEDĀNTA   The systematic exposition of the VEDA. Differences of
interpretation give rise to different systems of theology (e.g.
those of ŚAṄKARA and RĀMĀNUJA) which claim to be the
correct exposition, of the Veda.

VEDĀNTIN   Pertaining to the VEDĀNTA.

VEDIC   Pertaining to the VEDA or to the religion expressed therein.

VIDYĀ   Metaphysical or spiritual knowledge or insight. See
AVIDYĀ.

VIṢṆU   One of the two great gods of devotional Hinduism. Though an unimportant figure in VEDIC religion, Viṣṇu acquired, with ŚIVA, a dominant position in the period following that of the early UPANIṢADS. Associated with Viṣṇu is the conception of AVATĀRA, Viṣṇu appearing on earth in various animal and human forms, the most famous being KRISHNA. With BRAHMĀ, Viṣṇu and Śiva form a trinity and represent the way in which the Divine Being is variously manifested.

VISUDDHIMAGGA   *The Path of Purity*. See PATH OF PURITY.

YOGA   One of the traditional Indian metaphysical systems, closely associated with SĀṄKHYA, from which it derives its fundamental ideas. But it differs from Sāṅkhya in stressing the need for meditative practices in order to attain liberation, and also in elevating one of the souls (*puruṣas*) into the position of Supreme Soul or Lord (ĪŚVARA) who assists other souls towards liberation. But it should be noted that isolation from matter is the ultimate objective, *not* union with the *Īśvara*. The meditative practices can be divided into physical and mental ones, the former being a preparation for the latter. The term *yoga* is also used more generally for any such system of meditation (e.g. we can speak of Buddhist *yoga*, etc.).

YOGĀCĀRA   A philosophical school of Buddhism, arising out of the MĀDHYAMIKA, from which it differs (1) in emphasizing the need for *yoga* in order to attain to final truth; and (2) in adopting an idealist position in regard to reality—the Absolute being conceived as Absolute Mind, in line with the description of the highest states of trance as being the realization of pure consciousness.

INDEX